REVISE BTEC TECH AWARD
Enterprise

REVISION GUIDE

Series Consultant: Harry Smith

Author: Stephen Jakubowski

A note from the publisher

While the publishers have made every attempt to ensure that advice on the qualification and its assessment is accurate, the official specification and associated assessment guidance materials are the only authoritative source of information and should always be referred to for definitive guidance.

This qualification is reviewed on a regular basis and may be updated in the future. Any such updates that affect the content of this Revision Guide will be outlined at **www.pearsonfe.co.uk/BTECchanges**. The eBook version of this Revision Guide will also be updated to reflect the latest guidance as soon as possible.

> **For the full range of Pearson revision titles across KS2, KS3, GCSE, Functional Skills, AS/A Level and BTEC visit:**
> www.pearsonschools.co.uk/revise

Published by Pearson Education Limited, 80 Strand, London, WC2R ORL.

www.pearsonschoolsandfecolleges.co.uk

Text and illustrations © Pearson Education Ltd 2018
Typeset and illustrated by QBS Learning
Produced by QBS Learning
Cover illustration by Miriam Sturdee

The right of Stephen Jakubowski to be identified as author of this work has been asserted by him in accordance with the Copyright, Designs and Patents Act 1988.

First published 2018

21 20 19
10 9 8 7 6

British Library Cataloguing in Publication Data

A catalogue record for this book is available from the British Library

ISBN 978 1 292 24560 7

Printed in Slovakia by Neografia

Acknowledgements
The author and publisher would like to thank the following individuals and organisations for permission to reproduce photographs:

Shutterstock: zhu difeng 1, photocritical 49. **Alamy Stock Photo:** Richard Levine 2, Fotomatador 24, Blend Images 37.

Notes from the publisher

1. While the publishers have made every attempt to ensure that advice on the qualification and its assessment is accurate, the official specification and associated assessment guidance materials are the only authoritative source of information and should always be referred to for definitive guidance.

Pearson examiners have not contributed to any sections in this resource relevant to examination papers for which they have responsibility.

2. Pearson has robust editorial processes, including answer and fact checks, to ensure the accuracy of the content in this publication, and every effort is made to ensure this publication is free of errors. We are, however, only human, and occasionally errors do occur. Pearson is not liable for any misunderstandings that arise as a result of errors in this publication, but it is our priority to ensure that the content is accurate. If you spot an error, please do contact us at resourcescorrections@pearson.com so we can make sure it is corrected.

Websites
Pearson Education Limited is not responsible for the content of any external internet sites. It is essential for tutors to preview each website before using it in class so as to ensure that the URL is still accurate, relevant and appropriate. We suggest that tutors bookmark useful websites and consider enabling students to access them through the school/college intranet.

Introduction

Revising Component 3 of your BTEC Tech Award

This Revision Guide has been designed to support you in preparing for the externally assessed component of your course.

Component 3, Promotion and Finance for Enterprise, builds on the knowledge, understanding and skills developed in Components 1 and 2. The assessment requires you to analyse and interpret information in relation to an enterprise and to make recommendations on strategies to use to improve the performance of the enterprise.

Your Revision Guide

This Revision Guide contains two types of pages, shown below.

Content pages help you revise the essential content you need to know for Component 3.

Skills pages help you prepare for your assessment.

Skills pages have a coloured edge and are shaded in the table of contents.

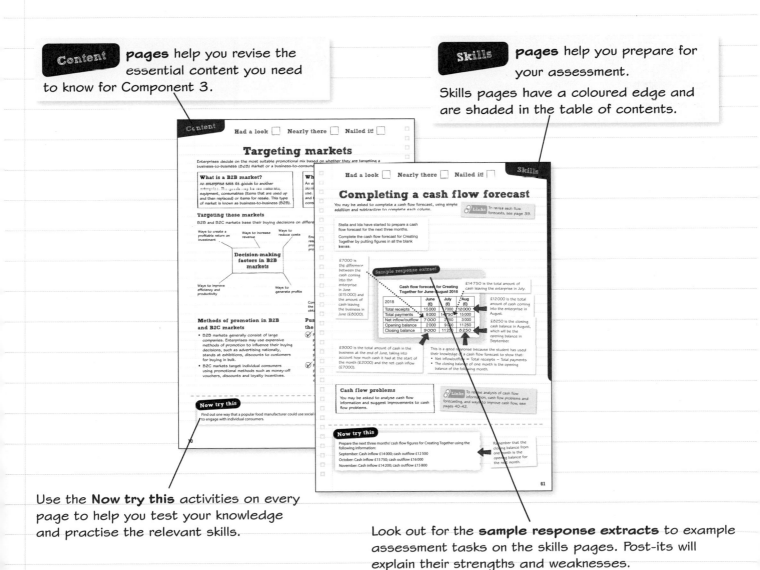

Use the **Now try this** activities on every page to help you test your knowledge and practise the relevant skills.

Look out for the **sample response extracts** to example assessment tasks on the skills pages. Post-its will explain their strengths and weaknesses.

Contents

A small bit of small print

Pearson publishes Sample Assessment Material and the Specification on its website. This is the official content and this book should be used in conjunction with it. The questions in *Now try this* have been written to help you test your knowledge and skills. Remember: the real assessment may not look like this.

The promotional mix

The purpose of most enterprises is to sell goods and services – their products. To attract customers, enterprises promote their products so that everyone who is likely to buy the products knows about them. The **promotional mix** is the different methods of communication that an enterprise uses to attract customers.

What is promotion?

Promotion is any method of communication that tries to encourage current and potential customers to buy products. Examples include adverts on television and money-off coupons in magazines.

The purpose of promotion

Promotion can be used to:

- create a positive image of the enterprise in the minds of current and potential customers
- encourage current and potential customers to buy products.

The promotional mix

There are many different methods of promotion used to get current and potential customers to buy products. Enterprises will choose a combination of methods depending on their product and their suitability for **the size of the enterprise**. This is known as the promotional mix.

You need to know the features of each element of the promotional mix and how they can benefit an enterprise.

Direct marketing   Advertising   Sales promotion

Methods of promotion

Public relations   Personal selling

Elements of the promotional mix

🔗 **Links** To revise each element of the promotional mix, see pages 2–9.

Target markets

Enterprises identify which groups of people are most likely to buy their products – their **target markets**. They choose the promotional mix based on the best way to reach their target markets.

The purpose of this promotion is to attract both current and potential customers.

Now try this

Consider **two** different products, such as trainers and headphones. Compare the methods of promotion used for each.

◀ Choose products targeted at different groups of people.

Advertising: message and medium

Advertising is an important element of the promotional mix. It is based on the **message** and the **medium**.

```
        Advertising
       /            \
The message      The medium
```

The message
What the communication needs to say

The medium
How to get the message across to current and potential customers – the target market

Purpose of advertising

The two main purposes of advertising are to:

* inform
* persuade.

The purposes are linked – once potential customers know about a product or service, they may be more likely to buy it.

The message

This is what an enterprise wants to tell current and potential customers about its product.

Key features of the message may include:

* Low price
* Good quality
* Healthy
* Lifestyle
* Fashionable
* Innovative
* Useful
* Tasty

The medium

This is the means of advertising that the enterprise uses to reach current and potential customers. In other words, it's how the enterprise chooses to get its message across. For example, a large enterprise may advertise its products on television while a small, local enterprise may put leaflets through letterboxes.

Depending upon the medium, the message can be conveyed through words, pictures, graphics, sounds and moving images.

Advertising as a reminder

While the overall aim of advertising is to persuade someone to purchase, there can be occasions when advertising has a third purpose – to remind people to do something (for example, how to stay fit and healthy). Government advertising campaigns aimed at those people who drink and smoke seek to *inform* them of the risks of drinking and smoking and try to *persuade* them to reduce the amount of alcohol they drink and to give up smoking. However, sometimes it isn't easy to persuade people to change their habits even when they are informed of potential dangers.

Now try this

What is the target market for the above advert, and what message is being conveyed? Think about the characteristics of the product.

Advertising: methods

Enterprises select from a variety of methods to advertise their products. Their choice depends on a number of factors.

Method of advertising	Where advertising appears	Benefits
Moving image	Television Cinema Video sites Promotional DVDs	👍 Enables products with moving parts or a practical use to be seen in action and where/how they can be used
Print	Local and national newspapers Magazines Leaflets Billboards	👍 Likely to be seen by large numbers of people, either in a specific location (local newspaper, billboards and leaflets) or over a wide geographical area (national newspapers and magazines)
Ambient	Public places, such as bus stops, shopping centres	👍 Outdoor advertising aims to catch the attention of passers-by
Digital	Company websites Social media, such as Pinterest or Instagram	👍 Enables large and small businesses to connect with large numbers of people instantly
Audio	Local and national radio	👍 Allows businesses to speak directly to their target market

Which advertising method?

Enterprises are influenced by different factors when choosing which advertising method is most suitable to promote their product.

Type of product
How best to promote a product's features

Potential sales that could result from the advert. An enterprise will want to get a financial return from its investment in advertising

Factors which influence choice of advertising method

Characteristics of target market
Factors such as income, gender, age and lifestyle will influence the method used to attract customers

Cost
Some methods, such as television advertising, can be very expensive and may only be suitable for large enterprises with big advertising budgets. Other methods, such as leaflets, may offer better value, particularly for small, local enterprises that may not have much to spend on advertising

Now try this

A small enterprise is considering whether to use a radio advert to promote a product to 16–20-year-olds. What factors should it take into account?

Think about costs, characteristics of the target market and potential sales.

3

Sales promotion: purpose and methods

All promotional activities aim to get products known in their target market. **Sales promotion** is specifically designed to boost sales. It involves offering an incentive to persuade current and potential customers to buy products.

Purpose of sales promotion

Enterprises use sales promotion for different reasons.

To entice people into a shop where they may buy not only the product but other products that are not in the sales promotion

To attract first-time buyers who may become loyal customers having tried a product or brand

To sell off older or less-fashionable goods to make space for new items

Purpose of sales promotions

To boost sales figures, particularly where a local enterprise is ranked on its monthly sales

To maintain customer loyalty

Methods of sales promotion

These are the main methods used by enterprises to promote their products to customers:

Method and features	Benefits/limitations
Coupons Money-off voucher	👍 May encourage the customer to buy the product rather than a rival product 👎 Impacts on profit if money-off price doesn't cover costs of product
Free sample Often given with discount coupon (try before you buy)	👍 Having tried the product, customers may decide to buy (possibility of repeat sales) – increases profit 👎 Impacts on profit if too few sales generated
Competitions Prize draws, for example for a free holiday, cash prize or free products	👍 Allows the enterprise to build up marketing information as customers provide details to enter competitions; appeals to people's sense of thrill to build interest in the product 👎 Impacts on profit
Money off/discounts A percentage reduction on the original price	👍 Encourages customers to buy more products 👎 Impacts on profit if too few sales generated
Loyalty incentive Loyal customers obtain points on purchases that can either be put towards other products or they get something for free	👍 Establishes a long-term relationship with customers; customers may choose the enterprise's products over a rival's 👎 Impacts on profit if too few sales generated
Buy one get one free (BOGOF) A free product when a full-priced product is purchased	👍 May encourage customers to buy additional products as they have saved money elsewhere 👎 Impacts on profit if too few sales generated

Now try this

Lisa has started her own business selling greeting cards online. Identify **three** factors she should take into account when deciding which sales promotion methods to use.

 This is a new business with limited resources.

4

Sales promotion: choosing methods

Enterprises will be influenced by several factors when choosing the most suitable sales promotion methods.

Size of enterprise

Large enterprises with a large customer base may have the financial resources to use sales promotion methods which impact on profit. Smaller organisations may not be able to afford the cost of free samples, competitions or money-off vouchers. Their scope for sales promotion may be more limited.

Type of product

Some methods of sales promotion are more suitable than others depending on the product. For example, money-off vouchers and free samples are more suitable for lower priced products, while buy one get one free would be inappropriate for expensive or luxury items, such as a car.

The product lifecycle

The cost of sales promotions can reduce profits, so enterprises need to decide the most suitable times to use them. During the lifecycle of a product – as the product passes from development and launch to when it is removed from the market – incentives may be used to increase sales or encourage customer loyalty.

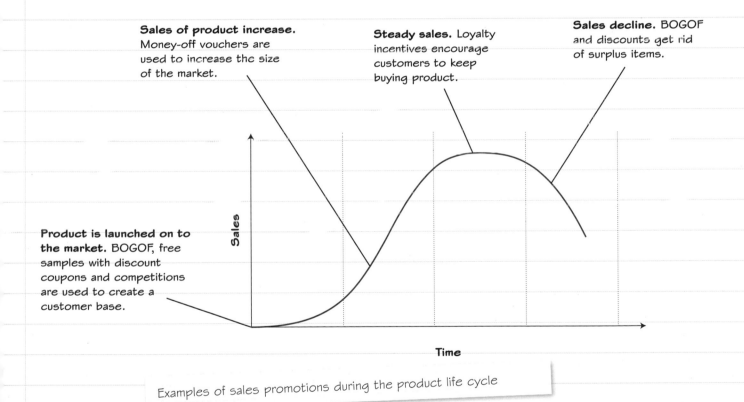

Sales of product increase. Money-off vouchers are used to increase the size of the market.

Steady sales. Loyalty incentives encourage customers to keep buying product.

Sales decline. BOGOF and discounts get rid of surplus items.

Product is launched on to the market. BOGOF, free samples with discount coupons and competitions are used to create a customer base.

Sales

Time

Examples of sales promotions during the product life cycle

Now try this

Recommend the sales promotion methods which could be used in the following situations:

(a) A large sports clothing retailer wants to sell off old stock and promote its new product line.

(b) A mobile phone provider is launching a brand new range of smartphones.

Consider the type of product, product lifecycle and size of enterprise.

Choosing promotional methods

Enterprises consider a number of factors when selecting which promotional methods to use. They include the size of the enterprise, its promotional budget (the money it has to spend), the type of product and how best to attract the attention of the target market.

Large enterprises

These are likely to:

- have a large promotional budget
- use all of the promotional methods you have revised
- employ specialist staff to plan and manage promotional methods
- employ a team of sales staff to promote products
- hire public relations specialists and agencies to promote the brand.

Smaller enterprises

These are likely to have:

- a limited promotional budget
- a narrower range of promotional methods as some would be too costly.

They are unlikely to employ specialist staff. Promotions may only run at certain times to keep costs down. These may be linked to the skills of the owner and employees, the type of products, the size of the market and the budget.

The promotional budget

Both large and small enterprises set aside money to run promotional activities.

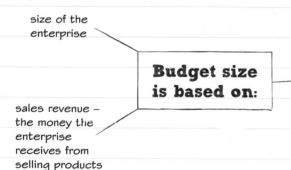

size of the enterprise

sales revenue – the money the enterprise receives from selling products

Budget size is based on:

how much competition there is – enterprises may spend more on promotion where there are lots of competitors

Budgetary constraints

- Promotional methods may be limited in scope for smaller enterprises with small budgets.
- Decisions on spending may be influenced by product lifecycle. For example, new products may require a bigger budget than a product with steady sales.
- Poorly performing enterprises may have to restrict promotional activities to those that generate most sales.

Type of product

Enterprises need to choose methods that are appropriate for the product. For example:

- A large car manufacturer may use a wide range of promotional methods (television, radio, social media, newspaper and magazine adverts).
- A small local internet café may simply use leaflets or word of mouth.
- A product with complicated features or different levels of service, such as double-glazing or cable TV subscriptions may be sold by a sales team.
- A product with health benefits could be promoted by PR activities.

Target market

To have a positive impact on sales, promotional methods must:

- reach the target market
- entice customers to buy
- be based upon the habits of the target group, including what they read, their lifestyle and their use of social media.

Now try this

Identify **three** ways in which a small enterprise could reduce the amount of money it spends on promotional leaflets.

 The level of its sales revenue should not be affected.

Personal selling

Personal selling is where a representative of an enterprise contacts potential customers directly – either face to face, by telephone, email or video conferencing. Large enterprises may employ a specialist sales team. The advantages and disadvantages of each method of personal selling are outlined below.

Face to face

The salesperson is in direct personal contact with the customer.

👍 Able to watch customer's facial expressions/body language and adapt the sales message to suit customer's needs

👍 Can answer customer's questions instantly

👎 Requires a high level of interpersonal skills

👎 Can be time-consuming and therefore expensive.

Telephone

The salesperson makes phone calls to the customer (usually from a call centre).

👍 Able to contact customers anywhere at a time that is convenient

👍 Can answer questions instantly

👎 Unable to respond to customer's body language or facial expressions

👎 Lots of customers may not answer the call making it a less efficient method.

Email

The salesperson communicates electronically with the customer.

👍 Can send customer web links and additional information and sales brochures in email attachments

👎 Impersonal

👎 May take longer than a face-to-face conversation

👎 No guarantee that initial email will be read by customer.

Video or web conferencing

The salesperson communicates with the customer through a webcam.

👍 Able to watch customer's facial expressions/body language and respond instantly

👍 Can access customers around the world

👎 Customer can watch product being demonstrated but unable to try it out themselves

👎 Requires access to webcam facilities.

Stages in the personal selling process

These stages can be an effective way of promoting products that have many features or are complicated as it allows the sales person to demonstrate the product and answer the customer's questions.

1 Lead generation Identify potential customers (find leads). ▷ **2 Qualify leads** Is customer interested? Can they afford it? ▷ **3 Demonstrate solutions and value** Show how product meets needs and interests of customer. ▷ **4 Manage objections** Answer queries and concerns about product, features and price. ▷ **5 Deliver and support** Deliver product and provide excellent after-sales service.

Now try this

Identify the qualities required to be an effective salesperson.

◀ Think about both personal qualities and technical knowledge a salesperson may require.

Public relations

An enterprise's public image is an essential aspect of its success. A poor reputation may lead to reduced sales and a fall in profits. A positive image can maintain or even increase sales. Public relations (PR) involves building and maintaining an enterprise's reputation – its image – through the media.

The purpose of public relations

PR may be used to promote products. Its purpose is to:

- encourage positive views of the enterprise among the general public and other organisations
- encourage positive publicity through the media
- protect or enhance the brand image.

Media space generated by PR activities is different from direct advertising.

> ### Brand image
> A set of beliefs and opinions associated with a product, service or enterprise in the minds of consumers.

Public relations methods

PR activities aim to get the enterprise positive publicity without paying for the time or media space directly.

Press release
- A 150–200-word article produced by an enterprise and sent to news agencies highlighting something newsworthy or interesting about a new or existing product or service
- Covers the five Ws – who, what, when, where, why; may include a photo

Exhibitions
- Commercial events where many similar enterprises exhibit their products or explain the services they offer
- Newsworthy stories may be publicised by local and national news

Public relations activities

Sponsorship
- Enterprises pay to have their name and brand displayed at major events, such as a sporting venue
- Celebrities are sponsored (paid) to publicise an enterprise's goods and services – celebrity endorsements
- Enterprises associate themselves with a good cause, such as a charity

> ### Promotional stunts
> Some enterprises use one-off publicity stunts to catch the attention of the media and general public. For example, when some customers were unable to buy Virgin Train's newly launched 26–30 Railcard due to a website crash, they were invited to bring an avocado when booking their tickets. By simply showing their avocado, they were able to claim the same discount offered by the card!

Benefits and limitations of PR

 Free positive publicity from a neutral source such as a newspaper.

 Reaches a wide audience.

 Improve brand image and sales.

👎 Enterprise has no control over how journalists may write up the story – If story is 'negative', consumers may not want to be associated with the brand image.

👎 News story may not be picked up by media.

👎 Difficult to measure impact on reputation.

Now try this

A small restaurant has been asked to support a local charity's fund-raising event including a raffle. Recommend **three** ways the restaurant could support the event to generate positive local publicity.

 Consider both financial and non-financial support.

Direct marketing

Direct marketing is when an enterprise communicates with a customer directly to try to sell them something, either by phone or written communication.

The purpose of direct marketing

Direct marketing enables an enterprise to set up an individual relationship with the customer. Since the enterprise already knows its target market, it is able to tailor the message being sent to the customer to meet their needs. The enterprise must have the customer's postal address, telephone number or email address in order to contact them.

Benefits and limitations of direct marketing

👍 Can build positive associations with a brand, leading to repeat sales.

👍 May introduce new customers to products.

👎 Uninvited phone calls may be unwelcome.

👎 Customers may ignore written communication.

Methods of direct marketing

Direct mail (junk mail):
leaflets, letters and brochures about new products. Suitable for a small enterprise such as a local restaurant or service

Mail order catalogues:
include photos and descriptions of products and information on how to order. Used by enterprises selling a wide range of products, such as building materials, tools or clothing

Magazines:
- enterprise's own magazine including features and news of its latest products
- specialist magazines targeting a specific market
Usually used by large established enterprises with a large customer base such as supermarkets or financial institutions

Methods of direct marketing

Telemarketing:
sales representatives make phone calls to inform customers of offers or new products (cold calling). Suitable for an enterprise selling home improvements such as double-glazing

Email marketing and text messaging:
both may include links to the enterprise's website. Used by enterprises with a major online presence, such as specialist hotel booking companies, or whose customers have a track record of online shopping

Now try this

Summertime Garden Centres operates a chain of garden centres in major towns and cities selling a wide range of plants, gardening equipment and garden furniture. It also offers a 24/7 online shopping service and a 'Gardeners Enquiry Service'. Recommend **three** methods of direct marketing it could use.

Consider the methods that will reach the largest number of customers.

Targeting markets

Enterprises decide on the most suitable promotional mix based on whether they are targeting a business-to-business (B2B) market or a business-to-consumer market (B2C).

What is a B2B market?

An enterprise sells its goods to another enterprise. The goods may be raw materials, equipment, consumables (items that are used up and then replaced) or items for resale. This type of market is known as business-to-business (B2B).

What is a B2C market?

An enterprise sells its products – goods and services – directly to individuals for their own use. Such individuals are known as consumers, and the type of market is known as business-to-consumer (B2C).

Targeting these markets

B2B and B2C markets base their buying decisions on different factors.

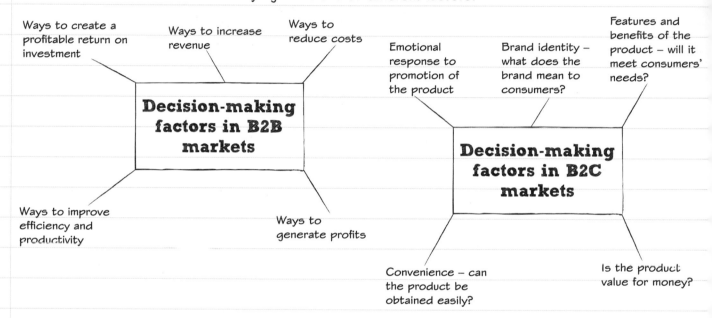

Methods of promotion in B2B and B2C markets

- B2B markets generally consist of large companies. Enterprises may use expensive methods of promotion to influence their buying decisions, such as advertising nationally, stands at exhibitions, discounts to customers for buying in bulk.

- B2C markets target individual consumers using promotional methods such as money-off vouchers, discounts and loyalty incentives.

Push and pull strategies in the B2B market

✓ Pull strategy: enterprises promote the product directly to consumers to create demand, for example through television advertising. The B2B market then buys the product as a consumer market has been built up for it.

✓ Push strategy: enterprises promote the product directly to the B2B market, for example giving an incentive such as a discount for buying large quantities.

Now try this

Find out one way that a popular food manufacturer could use social media to engage with individual consumers.

 Use an internet search engine to complete your research.

Segmenting the market

Markets can be sorted into different sections, known as segments. Each segment is made up of consumers with shared characteristics, needs and interests. Enterprises segment their markets for various reasons.

Market segmentation

This is the process of breaking down a large market into much smaller groups of consumers.

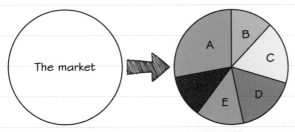

Enterprises analyse the market, and divide it into segments, each containing consumers with similar characteristics.

Process of market segmentation

Why enterprises segment the market

- To better understand the characteristics, needs and interests of current and potential customers
- To develop products that suit the needs of different market segments
- To develop products for a particular market segment
- To choose promotional methods that are better suited to the target market.

Features of segmented markets

Markets can be segmented in different ways. Enterprises may target one or more segments. They may also target different categories within each segment.

Demographic segmentation covers various characteristics of consumers, such as age, gender, family size, ethnicity/race, religious and cultural beliefs, income, education level, socio-economic group

Geographic segmentation is where consumers live

Market segments

Behavioural segmentation includes consumer spending choices, how often customers buy products (usage rate) and the benefits consumers expect to get from them, and how loyal consumers are to brands and enterprises

Psychographic segmentation includes social class, attitudes, lifestyle, personality characteristics

- -

Now try this

Identify the different segments of the new car market that would influence the promotion of electric cars.

 Electric motor cars currently tend to be more expensive than other types of motor vehicles and do not have a long mileage range.

Demographic and geographic segments

Segmenting a market by demographics allows enterprises to focus their products and promotional methods on shared population characteristics. Geographic segmentation allows enterprises to focus on the needs of consumers in different areas.

Demographics

Gender
Men and women have different tastes, interests and needs. Toiletry products are often segmented by gender

Age
People's tastes, interests and needs may change at different life stages. Markets are often segmented by different age ranges, such as 18–24-year-olds or over-50s. Holidays are an example of a product targeted at different age groups

Income
People with higher incomes may have money to spend on luxury brands, such as designer clothing and jewellery

Education level
People with a higher level of education may earn more and spend their extra income on a wide range of cultural interests

Population characteristics

Family size
Larger families usually buy products such as food and washing powder in bigger quantities. Family-size packs are marketed to this segment. Tour operators market group holidays for single people

Ethnicity, religious and cultural beliefs
These may influence people's choice of food, clothing and cultural preferences. Some specialist food manufacturers target their products at specific communities

Socio-economic group
People's social class is based on their income and type of occupation. Luxury cars are an example of a product that may be targeted at social class AB, which includes people in senior managerial positions

Geographic segmentation

Where people live influences the products they buy. For example:

- People living in cold, hot or damp climates will need different types of clothing and transport.
- Regional tastes in cuisines mean different demands for food.
- Customs and cultural characteristics of a country or region affect people's choices.
- The general standard of living in an area will affect how much consumers have to spend.

Promoting the product

Vialli's, a new local Italian restaurant and takeaway, has focused on demographic and geographic segments:

- ✓ Discounts are offered to over-60s on weekday lunchtimes, and family groups at weekends.
- ✓ On Tuesdays, customers buying a large takeaway pizza receive a second small pizza free.

Now try this

Recommend a promotional method that could be used by Vialli's Italian restaurant and a way the restaurant could be promoted to attract younger customers.

 Think about the costs and impact of the promotional methods.

Psychographic and behavioural segments

Markets can be segmented according to consumers' attitudes, lifestyles and opinions. This is known as psychographic segmentation. Behavioural segmentation looks at how consumers relate to products through spending and consumption, usage, loyalty and desired benefits. Both segments impact on promotional methods used by enterprises.

Psychographic segmentation

Consumers are segmented by:

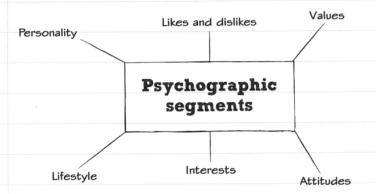

Personality
Likes and dislikes
Values
Psychographic segments
Lifestyle
Interests
Attitudes

Using psychographic segmentation

✓ Cinemas may offer two-for-one deals, discounts and annual passes to attract regular movie-goers and encourage customer loyalty.

✓ Products made of sustainable resources, that can be recycled, and do not use animal products may be promoted to meet the needs of environmentally conscious consumers.

Spending and consumption

When deciding what promotional methods to use, enterprises take into account how much money consumers have available to spend. Spending and consumption can be affected by how well the country's economy is doing. If the level of inflation or unemployment is high, promotional methods may focus on value for money, including price discounts and special offers.

Usage rate

This measures how regularly customers buy products. Promotional methods may include:

- For low-value products, such as drinks, loyalty cards reward regular customers with a free product once they have bought a certain number.

- For high-value products, such as air travel, frequent flyer programmes may offer regular customers points that can be exchanged for free flights or free upgrades.

Loyalty

To encourage customers to keep buying their products, enterprises may offer loyalty cards. These can be used to obtain information on a customer and to personalise promotions, such as special offers on specific products which are purchased regularly by the customer. Enterprises may also text or email regular and past customers with news of latest products, offers and discounts.

Desired benefits

Products have features that provide benefits to customers or meet their needs. For example, car manufacturers may target their promotion depending on what customers require, such as electric cars for environmentally conscious drivers or small cars for driving in towns and cities.

Now try this

Identify the psychographic characteristics associated with consumers who may be attracted to buying a new low-sugar, high-energy sports drink.

Consider aspects such as personality, values, interests and lifestyle.

Financial documents

Enterprises use a range of financial documents throughout the buying and selling process to record the sale and purchase of goods and services.

Examples of common financial documents

 Purchase order → Delivery note → Invoice → Receipt → Credit note → Statement of account

Purchase order

- Completed by buyer (the customer)
- A legal offer to buy goods from supplier
- Lists items required, including price agreed and quantity
- Sent to supplier requesting products.

Documents are linked

Financial documents used in the buying and selling process connect with each other.

Invoice

- Completed by supplier
- A request for payment – sent to customer, either on receipt of goods or shortly after
- Lists price of goods delivered, delivery charges and amount owed to supplier
- States date by which money must be paid
- Explains how to pay, for example by bank transfer.

Credit note

- Completed by supplier and sent to customer
- Lists any goods that may have been returned by the customer
- Confirms money refunded to customer or may be used against the purchase of other goods by customer in the future.

Delivery note

- Completed by supplier
- Sent to customer when goods delivered
- Lists details about the order, including contents of delivery
- Lists any goods not supplied, with reason for non-delivery
- Used by customer to check that goods delivered match goods requested on purchase order.

Receipt

- Completed by supplier and sent to customer
- A record of payment made by the customer
- Rarely used when enterprises sell goods on credit (see statement of account).

Statement of account

- Completed by supplier and sent to customer
- A financial summary of the goods ordered, purchased or returned by the customer over a period of time, usually a month
- Some enterprises pay their invoices only after receiving the statement.

Now try this

Explain the consequences for the supplier if a credit note was not completed accurately.

 Think about the purpose of a credit note.

Accuracy of financial documents

Financial documents provide a record of the trading and financial transactions taking place between the enterprise (the supplier) and its customers. All documents must be completed accurately.

Purpose of financial records

Enterprises use financial records for a range of purposes. They enable enterprises to run smoothly.

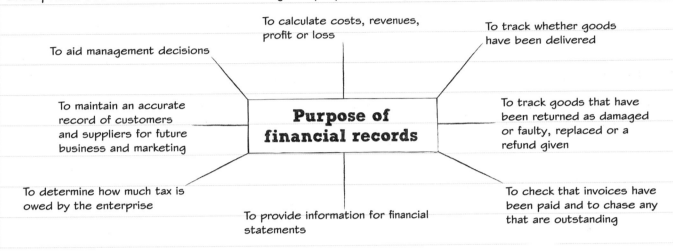

To aid management decisions

To calculate costs, revenues, profit or loss

To track whether goods have been delivered

To maintain an accurate record of customers and suppliers for future business and marketing

Purpose of financial records

To track goods that have been returned as damaged or faulty, replaced or a refund given

To determine how much tax is owed by the enterprise

To provide information for financial statements

To check that invoices have been paid and to chase any that are outstanding

The importance of accuracy

Here are some reasons why it's important for an enterprise to keep accurate financial records:

👍 To ensure the correct goods are delivered in the correct quantities to the right customer.

👍 To check that customers are not being overcharged or undercharged for goods.

👍 To ensure the enterprise has sufficient inventory (stock) to meet customer demand.

👍 To ensure calculations of costs and revenues are accurate.

👍 To ensure both enterprise and customer have a clear understanding of the terms of sale, including prices and delivery schedules.

👍 To enable the enterprise to accurately calculate the taxes it owes to the government.

👍 To allow managers to make strategic decisions.

Here are some of the problems with inaccurate financial records:

👎 Profits may be over- or understated.

👎 Not all costs are accounted for.

👎 Investors may lose confidence in the business.

👎 Reputation of the business can be damaged.

👎 Financial statements will not be accurate.

👎 It can lead to cash-flow problems.

👎 Suppliers and other trade payables may not be paid on time.

👎 Bad debts can increase.

Now try this

Suggest **two** ways an enterprise could reduce the risk of losing its financial records.

Think about paper records and electronic records.

Purchase order

The purchase order starts the buying and selling process. Financial documents, such as a purchase order, are usually completed on a pre-printed official form. Details of the goods to be ordered are normally found in the supplier's sales catalogue.

A completed purchase order

Below is a completed purchase order showing all the details that have been entered to calculate the cost of the order.

The customer sends a purchase order to the supplier.

Ensure name and contact details of supplier and buyer are filled in accurately.

Suppliers publish catalogues which list and describe the goods they sell. Each item will have a catalogue number or order code.

The supplier may offer discounts to loyal customers or on bulk orders.

Value added tax (VAT) is a government tax which is calculated as a percentage of the total cost of the order – the subtotal.

EatIn Pizzas PURCHASE ORDER

Purchase Order No. 031220

Date: 1/12/2018

To: Braddock Soft Drinks Ltd
Unit 10
Century Way
Anytown AN30 1XX

Deliver to: EatIn Pizzas
15 High Street
Anytown AN40 3YY

Tel: 01234 567890

Invoice to: EatIn Pizzas

Item description	Catalogue No.	Price per case £	Price per case p	Quantity	Total price £	Total price p
Lemonade	23478/LM	4	20	5	21	00
Orange	59352/OR	4	00	1	4	00
Goods total					25	00
Discount @ 10%					2	50
Subtotal					22	50
VAT @ 20%					4	50
Total to pay					27	00

The total amount to be paid by the buyer to the supplier.

Remember to fill in the date of the order.

This is the address of where the goods are to be sent.

The price of an item is usually listed before any discount.

Sometimes goods are purchased in specific quantities, such as a box or case of six items.

5 × £4.20 = £21.00

> £21.00 + £4.00 = £25.00

10% of £25.00 = £2.50

> £25.00 − £2.50 = £22.50

20% of £22.50 = £4.50

> £22.50 + £4.50 = £27.00 paid by the buyer.

EatIn Pizzas ordered a further seven cases of lemonade and four cases of orange from the supplier. The discount is 10 per cent. Using the catalogue details given in the purchase order, calculate the total to pay.

Remember to subtract the discount from the goods total first and then calculate the VAT on the subtotal.

Delivery note and invoice

Although the purchase order, delivery note and invoice have different purposes, the details on all three documents should match.

A completed delivery note

Below is a completed purchase order for the order shown on page 16.

The delivery note is sent by the supplier.

The delivery address and the invoice address should match those on the purchase order.

The details of the goods delivered should match those on the purchase order.

Braddock Soft Drinks

Unit 10, Century Way, Anytown AN30 1XX

DELIVERY NOTE

Delivery address: **Invoice address:**

EatIn Pizzas   EatIn Pizzas

15 High Street AN40 3YY   15 High Street AN40 3YY

Order Date: 1/12/2018

Order No: 031220   **Despatch date:** 4/12/2018

Catalogue No	Description	Ordered	Received	Signature
23478/LM	Lemonade	5	5	L. Kay
59352/OR	Orange	1	1	L. Kay

The delivery address and the invoice address should match those on the purchase order.

The customer signs the delivery note.

The actual number of items delivered should be checked and recorded by the customer.

A completed invoice

The full name of the supplier and customer appear on the invoice.

Braddock Soft Drinks

INVOICE

INVOICE No: 21672/EP

Date: 10/12/2018

To: EatIn Pizzas

Catalogue No	Description	Ordered	Price per case		Total cost	
			£	p	£	p
23478/LM	Lemonade	5	4	20	21	00
59352/OR	Orange	1	4	00	4	00
				Total	25	00
			Discount at 10%		2	50
			Total excluding VAT		22	50
			VAT @ 20%		4	50
			Total to pay		27	00
Terms: Invoice to be settled within 30 days						

A supplier may allow the business 30 days before the invoice has to be paid. This is known as **trade credit**.

Now try this

Why is it important to include the purchase order number on the delivery note?

Remember that a supplier may supply identical goods to a customer over a period of time.

17

Receipt and credit note

Below is a completed receipt and a credit note for the order shown on page 17.

A completed credit note

On the purchase order number 031220 the supplier delivered four boxes of lemonade and one box of cola in error instead of five boxes of lemonade. The box of cola was returned to the supplier who issued a credit note.

Braddock Soft Drinks

Unit 10, Century Way, Anytown AN30 1XX

CREDIT NOTE

EatIn Pizzas

15 High Street

Anytown AN40 3YY

Credit note date: 4/1/2019

Credit note number: 23451/CN

Catalogue No	Item	Unit	Unit price		Discount @10%		VAT @20%		Total	
			£	p	£	p	£	p	£	p
23478/LM	Lemonade	5								
59352/OR	Orange	1	4	20	3	78	0	76	4	54

This is the amount that will be credited to the customer's account.

A completed receipt

EatIn Pizzas paid Invoice No 21672/EP (£27.00) in full on 31/1/2018 and was sent the following receipt by the supplier. They can offset the value of a future invoice by £4.54 (the value of the credit note).

Braddock Soft Drinks

Unit 10, Century Way, Anytown AN30 1XX

RECEIPT No 34896/EP

Sent to: EatIn Pizzas   **Receipt date:** 31/1/18

Catalogue No	Description	Quantity	Price per case		Total cost	
			£	p	£	p
23478/LM	Lemonade	5	4	20	21	00
59352/OR	Orange	1	4	00	4	00
				Total	25	00
			Discount at 10%		2	50
			Total excluding VAT		22	50
			VAT @ 20%		4	50
			Total paid in full		27	00

This shows there is no more money owing on the invoice.

Now try this

Copy the receipt above without the goods details. Complete a new receipt for Invoice No 21672/EP which you prepared on page 17. The receipt was issued on 17/1/18 and the receipt number is 23657/EP.

You prepared Invoice No 21672 when you completed the Now try this question on page 17.

Payment methods

There are many different ways for enterprises and their customers to pay for goods and services. Depending on the type of financial transaction, some methods are more suitable than others.

Debit card

Issued by banks to their customers (account holders); card is linked directly to cardholder's bank account.

👍 Payment taken directly from cardholder's bank account at time of transaction.

👍 No need for cash.

👍 Can be used for payment up to the amount in the cardholder's bank account (including any authorised overdraft limit).

👍 Contactless cards (up to value of £30 per transaction) do not require use of a PIN.

👍 Can be used remotely via phone or online.

👎 Can be stolen.

Cash (notes and coins)

👍 Accepted in most places.

👎 May not be suitable for very large transactions.

👎 Not suitable for online purchases.

👎 Can be lost or stolen.

👎 Mistakes can be made during transactions, such as incorrect change being given.

Payment technologies

👍 Ecommerce transactions such as PayPal allow individuals and enterprises to transfer money between buyers and sellers.

👍 Electronic payments such as Faster Payments and CHAPs allow same-day payments from one bank account to another.

👍 Online customer accounts linked to ecommerce website stores customers' payment details – simple to make repeat purchases.

👍 Payment apps allow transactions to be completed using smartphone.

👎 Some payment technologies such as PayPal and CHAPs charge a fee.

Credit card

Issued by banks and financial companies.

👍 Card issuer pays at time of transaction – a loan to the cardholder.

👍 Cardholder receives short interest-free period on amount borrowed.

👍 Contactless cards (up to value of £30 per transaction) do not require use of a PIN.

👍 Can be used for any amount up to a limit set by the card issuer so the customer does not incur high credit card charges.

👎 Card issuer charges interest on the balance outstanding after the interest-free period.

👎 Cards are issued with a credit limit so that the cardholder is limited to the amount they can spend, regardless of their financial situation.

👎 Seller pays a fee to credit card company each time customer pays by card.

Direct debit

An instruction to a bank authorising a third party, such as an enterprise, to transfer money of varying amounts from a customer's account to its own bank account on an agreed date.

👍 Simple way to pay regular bills – deducted automatically from customer's bank account.

👍 Third party may vary amounts making it a flexible way to collect payments.

👎 Customer must have sufficient money in their bank account to cover payment, otherwise payment will not take place.

Cheque

A written order to pay a sum of money from a bank account to the payee (enterprise or individual). This method of payment is declining in popularity.

👍 More secure than cash.

👎 Needs to be paid directly into a bank so can be inconvenient.

👎 Cannot be used remotely or online.

👎 Takes several days to clear (make funds available).

👎 Most banks charge businesses for paying in cheques.

Now try this

Describe **two** differences between a credit card and a debit card.

Banks issue both types of card.

19

Choice of payment methods

The payment method used by customers is based on a number of factors. The methods chosen will have an impact on the enterprise's revenue.

Convenience
- Most customers choose a method of payment that suits their personal circumstances. Older customers, for example, may prefer to pay by cash or cheque while younger customers are likely to use payment technologies
- Credit cards and debit cards make it easy to pay for larger transactions where cash would not be suitable
- Direct debit allows customers to spread payment over a period of time

Safety and security
Customers want to know their money is safe when making a purchase. Some customers prefer not to carry cash or cards as they may be stolen

Cost
Some methods, such as credit cards, may require customers to pay a fee or a rate of interest

Factors influencing customer choice of payment methods

Ability to pay
Some customers may overspend and get into debt. For example, using a credit card allows the cardholder to delay payment, but they may have difficulty paying the credit card bill when it comes due

Lifestyle
The ability to pay remotely means goods and services can be purchased from almost anywhere in the world at any time of day or night

Technology
Some methods require access to technology such as smartphone, tablet or computer

Impact on enterprise

Enterprises recognise that in order to maximise sales of products they need to offer customers a range of payment options. These may involve additional costs and risks:

- cash – may be stolen; high levels of security are required
- credit cards and debit cards – card readers are required; fees are payable by the enterprise on credit card sales
- direct debit – customer may not be able to keep up regular payments, resulting in a loss of sales revenue
- payment technologies – requires investment in technology and for the enterprise to become a member of ecommerce schemes.

Now try this

Recommend a payment method in each of the following situations:
(a) Purchasing a sandwich from a café.
(b) Paying a monthly mobile phone bill.
(c) Purchasing a pair of designer trainers.

 Consider factors such as convenience and cost.

Income

Enterprises receive income (money) from the sale of goods and services and from assets.

Income from sales

This is the most common form of income. Income from sales is known as **revenue** or **turnover**.

Credit sales – from sales using a method of credit such as a credit card

Cash sales – from over-the-counter sales

Commission received – when an enterprise acts as an agent for another enterprise and receives a percentage of every sale

Main types of revenue

Maintenance contracts – when an enterprise agrees to regularly service a product, usually annually, to keep it in working order

Repairs – when an enterprise repairs or services a product previously purchased by a customer

Calculating revenue

Revenue = Sales × Price per unit

For example, a high-street mobile phone shop sells 15 phones at £600 per phone. Revenue is:

Sales (15) × Price per unit (£600) = £9000

Income from assets

An asset is something owned by an enterprise, such as property or equipment. An asset can be sold to generate income for the enterprise.

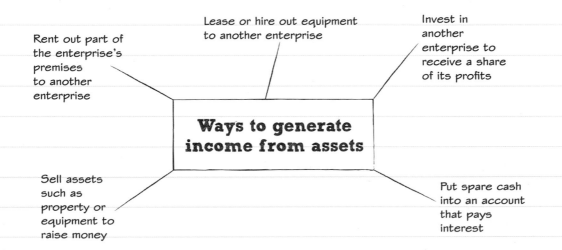

Rent out part of the enterprise's premises to another enterprise

Lease or hire out equipment to another enterprise

Invest in another enterprise to receive a share of its profits

Ways to generate income from assets

Sell assets such as property or equipment to raise money

Put spare cash into an account that pays interest

Now try this

Identify **three** ways a profitable local car dealership selling new cars could use its assets to generate income.

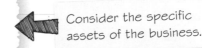

Consider the specific assets of the business.

Costs

Before an enterprise starts trading, it usually spends money on setting up. This is its **start-up costs**. Once an enterprise is trading, it will have day-to-day costs. These are its **running costs**.

Start-up costs

Start-up costs will be influenced by the type of enterprise. For example:

- A clothing manufacturer will require industrial premises, machinery and materials to produce goods.
- A high street retailer will require shop premises, shop fittings and items to sell.
- A service enterprise such as a car mechanic will require a garage premises, parts and tools.

Who pays start-up costs?

Before it earns any income, the enterprise has to find the finance to pay its start-up costs. Sources may include:

- owner's own money
- money loaned or given by family and friends
- business loan
- an investor.

Running costs

There are two main types of running costs.

```
           Running costs
          /            \
   Fixed costs      Variable costs
```

Fixed costs

These are costs that the enterprise has to pay no matter how well it is doing.

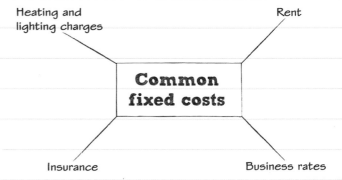

Heating and lighting charges — Rent — **Common fixed costs** — Insurance — Business rates

Variable costs

These costs are directly related to the number of items produced or sold. For example:

- The more orders a clothing manufacturer receives for T-shirts, the more material it will need to produce them.
- The more vehicles a car mechanic repairs and services, the more replacement parts will be required.

Total running costs

Together, **fixed costs** and **variable costs** make up the total running costs of the enterprise.

Total costs = Fixed costs + Variable costs

Running costs increase as a business grows in size. These costs must be paid for out of the increased income generated by the business.

Financial terminology

Enterprises keep track of their revenue and costs in order to prepare financial statements that they can analyse to understand how well they are performing. Financial statements use specialist terms which you will need to be familiar with. On this and the next few pages, you will revise the terminology used in financial statements.

Capital – money used to set up and then grow the business

Turnover – total revenue received by an enterprise in a given financial period

Cost of sales – cost of producing goods

Net current assets – value of current assets minus current liabilities

Creditors – individuals or enterprises, such as suppliers, that the enterprise owes money to

Debtors – individuals or enterprises that owe money to the enterprise

Financial terminology

Gross profit – turnover minus cost of sales

Expenses – indirect costs of the enterprise

Net profit – gross profit minus expenses

Fixed assets and current assets – things that the enterprise owns

Current liabilities and long-term liabilities – what the enterprise owes (including money) which must be paid back within a certain time period

Retained profit – net profit used to help the business grow

Understanding terminology

You may come across the terms below by different names elsewhere. The different terminology is shown in brackets – they mean the same thing:

- debtors (trade receivables)
- creditors (trade payables)
- fixed assets (non-current assets)
- long-term liabilities (non-current liabilities).

Financial terminology often appearing in financial statements

Statement of comprehensive income	Statement of financial position
Turnover	Fixed assets
Cost of sales	Current assets
Gross profit	Owner's capital
Expenses	Current liabilities
Net profit	Long-term liabilities (non-current liabilities)
Retained profit	Debtors (trade receivables)
	Creditors (trade payables)

Now try this

Identify one example of each of the following in relation to a manufacturer of sports trainers: **(a)** cost of sales, **(b)** expenses, **(c)** assets, **(d)** debtors, **(e)** creditors.

Cost of sales refers to the raw materials that are used to produce the goods.

Turnover, cost of sales and gross profit

Turnover is the total revenue received by an enterprise in a given financial period. The **cost of sales** Is the cost of producing goods. By subtracting the cost of sales from turnover, enterprises calculate their **gross profit**.

Turnover

Turnover is the value of sales generated by an enterprise from selling goods and services. Enterprises usually calculate turnover once a week, monthly and annually.

Sometimes an enterprise will offer its customers a discount on the price of its products. **Net sales** is the value of discounts minus the value of turnover.

Calculating turnover

Turnover = Price per item × Quantity sold

For example, a sports shop sells 500 pairs of running shoes, priced £42.50, a month. Its monthly turnover of running shoes is:

£42.50 × 500 = £21250

Gross profit

Gross profit is the money an enterprise makes from selling a product once cost of sales has been deducted.

Calculating gross profit

The formula for calculating gross profit is:
Gross profit = Turnover − Cost of sales

Cost of sales

Products cost money to make. This is the cost of sales. It is also known as **cost of goods sold**.

Cost of sales varies depending on the product made. It includes the cost of all the various items required to make a product. For example, the cost of sales of a ready meal will include the individual ingredients and the packaging. Cost of sales is calculated by adding together the cost of the individual items.

An enterprise may calculate the individual turnover of each of its products as well as total turnover of all the products it sells.

Eatin Pizza's sales revenue from pizza sales last year was £120000. Making the pizzas (the cost of sales) required pizza dough (£20000), tomato sauce (£10000), cheese (£15000) and toppings (£8000).

Gross profit was therefore:

= £120000 − (£20000 + £10000 + £15000 + £8000)
= £120000 − £53000
= £67000

Now try this

Jamie's Jeans makes children's jeans. It costs £8 to buy the raw materials for each pair of jeans. Jamie makes 175 pairs of jeans a month, and sells them at £20 per pair. In January, Jamie sold 175 pairs. In February, the business sold 100 pairs to one supplier, with a discount of 5 per cent, and 75 at the full price.

1 What is Jamie's cost of sales each month?

2 What was the turnover for January and February?

3 What is the gross profit for each month?

 Remember to calculate turnover and gross profit on the number of sales.

Profit and expenses

The term 'profit' is used to describe different aspects of the enterprise's finances. On page 24, you revised gross profit. On this page, you will revise net profit, retained profit and expenses. If gross profit or net profit is negative (a minus figure), the enterprise needs to take action.

Expenses

These are the indirect costs of the enterprise. They are not directly associated with making a product (cost of sales). Expenses may include:

- wages and salaries
- rent on premises
- heating and lighting
- delivery vehicles
- business insurance.

These are referred to as the enterprise's expenditure.

Net profit

This is the money remaining after deducting expenses (expenditure) from gross profit.

Calculating net profit

The formula for calculating net profit is:

Net profit = Gross profit − Expenditure

Retained profit

Net profit can be paid out to the owners of the enterprise or it may be kept within the enterprise as **retained profit**.

Retained profit can be used to finance the growth of the enterprise, for example by purchasing new machinery or moving into larger premises.

Calculating retained profit

The formula for calculating retained profit is:

Retained profit = Net profit − Amount of net profit paid to owners of enterprise

Gross profit: when to take action

- When gross profit is a positive (+) figure, the enterprise's revenue is greater than its cost of sales.
- When gross profit is low or negative (−), the enterprise needs to:
  - increase sales revenue – either by increasing the number of sales or prices of products
  - reduce cost of sales, for example by buying cheaper raw materials, buying in bulk, changing suppliers or negotiating discounts with existing suppliers.

Net profit: when to take action

- When net profit is positive (+), the enterprise will need to decide the amount to retain or spend.
- When net profit is negative (−), the enterprise needs to:
  - increase revenue from sales
  - reduce the cost of sales
  - reduce expenses.

Now try this

Explain how a business could increase its:

(a) gross profit

(b) net profit.

Consider revenue, costs of sales and expenses.

Fixed and current assets

An asset is something that an enterprise owns. Enterprises have two types of asset – fixed and current.

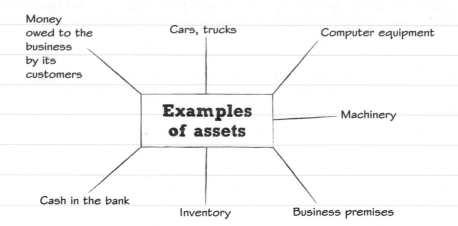

Money owed to the business by its customers — Cars, trucks — Computer equipment — **Examples of assets** — Machinery — Cash in the bank — Inventory — Business premises

Current assets

Current assets are either cash (money) or items that can be converted into cash very easily.

Types of current assets

Inventory:
- raw materials used to make products
- products held for future sales to customers

Cash: received from customers in payment for goods and deposited in the bank

Debtors: customers who owe money to the business

Calculating the value of current assets

The value of current assets can be calculated by adding together the value of the three types of current assets:

Current assets = Value of inventory + Cash at bank + Debtors

Fixed assets

A fixed asset is an item that enables products to be made and is not expected to be converted into cash any sooner than one year's time. Examples include:

- business premises owned by the enterprise
- fixtures and fittings
- computers and equipment
- vehicles.

Calculating the value of fixed assets

The value of fixed assets can be calculated by adding together the value of each fixed asset.

Calculating total assets

Total assets = Current assets + Fixed assets

Now try this

Calculate the value of a business's current and fixed assets from the following data: van £4000, inventory £2000, computers £2500, cash in bank £4000, money owed by customers £3250, other office equipment £2000.

Separate the assets out by identifying those items which are cash or easily converted into cash.

Liabilities, debtors and creditors

A liability is an amount of money owed by an enterprise. An enterprise will have two types of liabilities – current and long-term. The enterprise may owe money to its creditors and be owed money by its debtors.

Current liabilities

Current liabilities are short-term debts. The money owed must be paid back within one year. They may include:

- a bank overdraft (amount overspent on a current bank account)
- short-term loans (less than a year)
- money owed to suppliers for goods received (trade credit).

Long-term liabilities

Long-term liabilities are debts that are paid back over a long period of time. They may include:

- bank loans with a repayment period of more than one year
- mortgages taken out to finance the purchase of business premises, often paid back over 20 years
- the money originally invested in the business by the owner.

Calculating current liabilities

The value of current liabilities can be calculated by adding together the value of the enterprise's current (short-term) liabilities.

Calculating long-term liabilities

The value of long-term liabilities can be calculated by adding together the value of all the enterprise's long-term liabilities.

Debtors and creditors

The enterprise may owe money to its **creditors** – its suppliers. It may also be owed money by its **debtors** – its customers.

 Debtor – owes money to enterprise → Enterprise → Creditor – owed money by enterprise

Debtors

It's important for the enterprise to collect all the money it is owed from its debtors because it needs cash to pay its creditors. If debtors don't pay their debts, the business will suffer cash flow problems.

An enterprise will establish a **credit control system** to ensure that debtors pay their bills on time.

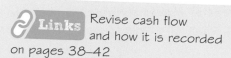 **Links** Revise cash flow and how it is recorded on pages 38–42

Creditors

Creditors can include those business who supply **goods** to the business – a car manufacturer, for example, will need to buy spare parts for the production line. It will also purchase **services** such as electricity and may have to pay back business **loans**.

If an enterprise does not pay its creditors, it could result in:

👎 suppliers refusing to supply spare parts or other goods

👎 services being cut off

👎 future business loans being difficult to obtain

👎 the enterprise being declared bankrupt.

Now try this

Calculate the value of the enterprise's short-term liabilities and its long-term liabilities from the following data: overdraft £2000, bank loan with three years still to pay £6000, short-term loan from business partner £1500, mortgage with 15 years still to pay £40000, trade credit £2500.

 First, identify the short-term and long-term liabilities.

Capital and net current assets

Capital is the amount of money put into an enterprise by the owner to start up the business so that it can begin trading. The net current assets total is the working capital of the business once it is established.

Capital

An enterprise requires resources to set it up. The money to purchase assets usually comes from the owner's funds. The enterprise may require additional capital in the form of a business loan. Retained profit can later be used as capital to grow the business.

Types of capital

Money invested in the enterprise by the owner (owner's capital)

Business loan

Retained profit

Net current assets

Current assets must always be greater than current liabilities. The different in value between the two is the enterprise's net current assets.

Calculating net current assets

Net current assets = Current assets – Current liabilities

When net current assets are positive

If the net current assets total is positive (+), the enterprise has money to pay its short-term debts (current liabilities).

When net current assets are negative

If the net current assets total is negative (–), the enterprise does not have the money to pay its current liabilities. This could result in financial difficulties.

Current assets £8000 | Net current assets +£1500 | Current liabilities £6500

Net current assets –£4000 | Current assets £6000 | Current liabilities £10000

Factors affecting the level of net current assets

The level of an enterprise's net current assets will reflect its methods of doing business and what it sells.

- Some enterprises need to hold stocks (inventory), such as finished goods or spare parts, which will be reflected in their current assets.

- Enterprises that only deal in cash sales will have few debtors (trade receivables), which will be reflected in their current liabilities.

- A small enterprise may have to pay suppliers straight away, whereas a large enterprise may be able to negotiate favourable trade credit terms with its suppliers so that it doesn't have to pay for supplies immediately.

- Some enterprises operate in markets where there is a seasonal demand for their products, which means that they purchase more stock at certain times of the year. This will be reflected in the level of their current assets (stocks lond debtors) and current liabilities (creditors).

- -

Now try this

Calculate an enterprise's net current assets from the following figures: current assets £7500, fixed assets £17 000, current liabilities £4500, long-term liabilities £12 250. Comment on your answer.

Is the net current asset value positive or negative?

Statement of comprehensive income

A statement of comprehensive income is a summary of the enterprise's activities over a specific period of time, usually a year. It is used by several interested groups of people to understand how well the enterprise is performing.

Statement of comprehensive income
1 January 2018–31 December 2018

	£	£
Sales revenue		15 400
Cost of sales		5 200
Gross profit		**10 200**
Less expenses		
Wages	2 800	
Rent	1 200	
Marketing	500	
Transport	1 800	
	6 300	
Net profit		3 900

This is the total of the individual expenses.

Sales revenue – this is the revenue received by the business from selling its products. It is also referred to as simply **sales** or **turnover** (net sales) because it takes into account any price discounts or goods returned by the customer

Cost of sales – this includes the cost of making the products.

Gross profit = Turnover – Cost of sales

Expenses – these are the indirect costs incurred when running a business. Expenses are listed separately in the statement of comprehensive income.

Net profit – once sales, cost of sales and expenses are identified, the net profit or loss can be calculated:
Net profit = Gross profit – Expenses.

Purpose of comprehensive statement of income

The financial statement shows:

- how much revenue the enterprise has received from sales of goods and services
- how much the enterprise has spent
- where the money was spent.

The enterprise will use the statement to understand how well it is performing in terms of costs, gross profit and net profit.

Interested groups

Several groups of people will be interested in the comprehensive statement of account as they will want to know that the enterprise is being well run. These stakeholders may include:

- managers
- employees
- shareholders (larger enterprises)
- suppliers
- customers
- tax authorities.

Why stakeholders are interested in the statement of comprehensive income?

- **Managers** will want to know if the enterprise has achieved its target turnover and profit levels for the year.
- **Employees** will want to know if their jobs are secure and if they are likely to receive a pay rise.
- **Shareholders** will expect a share of the profits.
- **Suppliers** will be able to determine if the business is financially sound.

- **Customers** want to be confident that the business is secure, particularly if they have paid for goods which will be delivered in the future.
- **The tax authorities** will be able to calculate the amount of tax owed by the business.

Now try this

Copy the statement of comprehensive income form above without the figures. Then complete a statement of comprehensive income for Savoury Rolls Ltd based on the following: sales of rolls £30 000; purchases of flour and fillings £6000; wages £10 000; rent £5000; marketing £1500; transport £1600; insurance £750.

Profit or loss

The information contained in the statement of comprehensive income can be used to calculate whether the enterprise has made a profit or a loss. If the enterprise has made a loss, it can decide what actions to take.

Profit

In the example of a statement of comprehensive income on page 29, both gross profit and net profit were positive figures, which means the enterprise made a profit.

Loss

If total costs (cost of sales + expenses) are greater than revenue, the enterprise will make a loss, as shown in the example below.

Statement of comprehensive income
1 January 2018–31 December 2018

	£	£
Sales revenue		15 400
Cost of sales		10 200
Gross profit		**5 200**
Less expenses		
Wages	2 800	
Rent	1 200	
Marketing	2 500	
Transport	1 800	
	8 300	
Net profit		(3 100)

Expenses are greater than gross profit. The enterprise has made a loss.

In financial statements, brackets are used to show when a figure is negative. The minus sign is not used.

Calculating profit or loss

Using the statement of comprehensive income, to calculate if an enterprise has made a profit or a loss, use this formula:

Gross profit = Sales revenue – Cost of sales

Net profit (or loss) = Gross profit – Expenses

Making a loss

An enterprise will need to take action if it makes a loss.

- Gross profit can be improved by increasing the volume of sales, reducing the cost of sale or increasing the price of products.

- Net profit can be improved by reducing expenses. In the example above, the enterprise could reduce the amount spent on marketing.

Now try this

Calculate a business's net profit from the following figures taken from its statement of comprehensive income: sales £35 450; cost of sales £12 250; expenses £8 400.

You need to calculate gross profit before you can calculate net profit.

Statement of financial position (1)

A statement of financial position is a financial snapshot of the assets and liabilities of an enterprise on a particular day, usually the last day of the enterprise's financial year.

Purpose of statement of financial position

This shows:

- the value of all of the enterprise's assets and liabilities
- the source of capital used by the enterprise to finance its operations.

Preparing a statement of financial position

To prepare a statement of financial position correctly, you first need to categorise the enterprise's assets into fixed and current assets, and its liabilities into current and long-term liabilities.

If you are unsure of any of the terms used in the statement of financial position below, you can revise them on pages 26–28.

Statement of financial position as of 31 December 2018

	£	£
Fixed assets		
Computer	500	
Vehicle	2000	
		2500
Current assets		
Inventory	4000	
Debtors	600	
Cash in bank	2000	
		6600
Current liabilities		
Creditors	700	
Overdraft	300	
		1000
Net current assets		5600
Total assets less current liabilities		8100
Financed by		
Owner's capital	5000	
Retained profit	3100	
		8100

This column identifies the *total value* of individual items.

This column includes the value of *individual items*.

The total fixed assets are £500 + £2000 = £2500

Total of current assets.

Total of current liabilities.

Net current assets = Current assets – Current liabilities = £6600 – £1000 = £5600

Owner's funds = Owner's capital + Net profit for the year = £5000 + £3100 = £8100 This figure will be reduced if the owner takes money out of the business to pay themselves a salary. It would be shown as 'Drawings'.

Now try this

Maisie is a decorator. Her van is worth £4000. She has an overdraft of £200 and owes her suppliers £800. She has £5000 in the bank. Customers owe her £300.

1 Identify one current liability.

2 Calculate Maisie's net current assets.

 First, identify Maisie's current assets and liabilities. Then do the calculation.

Statement of financial position (2)

You can find a lot of information about the enterprise in the statement of financial position. The information can be analysed to understand the enterprise's performance. From this, you can make suggestions to advise the enterprise on the actions it may need to take.

Net current assets (current assets – current liabilities)

Total assets owned by the enterprise (fixed assets + current assets)

Total liabilities owed by the enterprise (current liabilities + long-term liabilities)

Capital – shareholders' funds and retained profits

Information in the statement of financial position

Current assets – assets easily converted into cash

Long-term liabilities – debts that have to be paid over more than one year

Current liabilities – debts that need to be repaid within one year

Fixed assets – assets not easily converted into cash

Can the enterprise pay its short-term liabilities?

- **What to look for** – calculate the net current assets (current assets – current liabilities).

- **What it means** – if the net current assets figure is negative (–) the business may not have enough cash to pay its short-term debts.

- **Possible actions to take** – increase sales, reduce credit terms to customers, sell off fixed assets, reduce expenses.

What is the value of debtors?

- **What to look for** – debtors in current assets.

- **What it means** – if the figure is large compared with other current assets, there may be a risk that some customers will not pay the money they owe to the business.

- **Possible actions to take** – reduce the amount of trade credit provided to new customers; chase up customers who owe money.

Can the enterprise take a long-term loan to help grow the business?

- **What to look for** – the figure for long-term liabilities.

- **What it means** – if long-term liabilities are large, the business may find it difficult to get additional business finance.

- **Possible actions to take** – sell off fixed assets or use cash to pay off some long-term loans.

Has the enterprise made a profit?

- **What to look for** – the figure for retained profit.

- **What it means** – compare the figure with the retained profit from the previous year – has it increased or decreased?

- **Possible actions to take** – increase sales, reduce the cost of sales, reduce expenses.

Now try this

Copy the statement of financial position form on page 31 without the figures. Then complete a statement of financial position with the following information: computer £1000; vehicles £3000; inventory (stock) £45 000; debtors (trade receivables) £30 000 cash in bank £3000; creditors (trade payables) £34 000; overdraft £15 000. Comment on the financial position of the enterprise.

A statement of financial position identifies an enterprise's assets and liabilities.

Cash, profit, liquidity and profitability

Cash, profit, liquidity and profitability are all linked to the health of an enterprise. Analysing them will reveal whether an enterprise is solvent – able to pay its debts – or insolvent.

What is cash?

Cash is the money that an enterprise has. It is the coins and notes on the premises and money in the bank.

The value of an enterprise's cash appears in the statement of financial position as a current asset. It is the most liquid form of asset as it means the enterprise is able to pay its short-term debts. These debts include suppliers who may not be willing to continue to supply the enterprise, which could mean it will be unable to make a profit.

Liquidity

Liquidity is the ability of an enterprise to pay its debts.

👍 An enterprise with good (positive) liquidity will have sufficient net current assets to pay its creditors. It means the enterprise is **solvent** – can pay its debts.

👎 An enterprise with poor (negative) liquidity may not be able to pay its debts. The enterprise may become insolvent and have to cease trading.

Difference between cash and profit

Profit is what is left once all costs have been deducted from revenue. Figures for profit appear in the statement of comprehensive income.

Profit only becomes cash once the enterprise has received payment for its products. This could take several weeks.

Liquidity and cash

If an enterprise needs to pay debts in the near future – such as wages and heating and lighting – it will need to have access to cash. The ability of an enterprise to convert its assets into cash is known as its liquidity. For example, if a business has to pay its suppliers £5000 in 10 days' time but only has £2000 in cash, it could sell one of its fixed assets, such as a company vehicle it no longer requires, or sell some of its inventory (stock) at reduced prices.

What is profitability?

Profitability is the ability of an enterprise to turn revenue into profit. This is known as its **profit margin**. It is the amount of profit generated from each £1 generated in sales revenue. So, a profit margin of 20 per cent means the enterprise is generating £0.20 from each £1 of sales revenue.

Increasing profitability

An enterprise can increase its profitability by raising prices without demand falling or lower its costs without a noticeable change to the product or service.

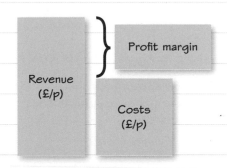

Profit margin from each £ of sales revenue – the size of profit margin will vary. A high profit margin means the enterprise will make a large profit.

Now try this

Why should an enterprise consider both its profit and profitability when reviewing its performance?

Consider both total profit and the profit made from each sale.

Profitability ratios (1)

A ratio compares one piece of information with another. In the case of the gross profit margin, the two pieces of information compared are the enterprise's gross profit and its turnover. The gross profit margin calculates gross profit as a percentage of sales revenue and shows what the gross profit is for every £ of sales.

Gross profit margin

To calculate gross profit margin, you will need to extract figures from the enterprise's statement of comprehensive income.

Formula for gross profit margin

Use this formula to calculate gross profit margin (GPM):

$$\text{Gross profit margin} = \frac{\text{Gross profit}}{\text{Sales revenue}} \times 100$$

The answer will be shown as a percentage.

Statement of comprehensive income for Revision Ltd

1 April 2018–31 March 2019

	£	£
Sales revenue		17 800
Cost of sales		7 120
Gross profit		10 680
Less expenses		
Wages	3 420	
Rent	1 400	
Marketing	600	
Insurance	1 700	
	7 120	
Net profit		3 560

Sales revenue and gross profit are the two items needed to calculate gross profit margin.

The values for sales revenue (£17 800) minus the cost of these sales (£7 120) will enable the business to calculate its gross profit.

Calculating gross profit margin

From the statement of comprehensive income for Revision Ltd above, the gross profit margin is calculated as follows:

$$\text{GPM} = \frac{\text{Gross profit}}{\text{Sales revenue}} \times 100$$

$$= \frac{10\,680}{17\,800} \times 100$$

$$= 60\%$$

Interpreting the gross profit margin

Revision Ltd has a gross profit margin of 60 per cent. For every £ it makes in sales, it generates £0.60 in gross profit.

If the gross profit margin falls, the enterprise may take steps to reduce its cost of sales or increase its sales revenue.

Now try this

Calculate the gross profit margin of a company with sales revenue of £20 800 and a gross profit of £16 640.

 Use the formula for GPM.

Profitability ratios (2)

The net profit margin is also a profitability ratio. It calculates net profit as a percentage of sales revenue and shows what the net profit is for every £ of sales.

Net profit margin

To calculate net profit margin, you will need to extract figures from the enterprise's statement of comprehensive income.

Formula for net profit margin

Use this formula to calculate net profit margin (NPM):

$$\text{Net profit margin} = \frac{\text{Net profit}}{\text{Sales revenue}} \times 100$$

The answer will be shown as a percentage.

Sales revenue and net profit are the two items needed to calculate net profit margin.

Statement of comprehensive income for Revision Ltd
1 April 2018–31 March 2019

	£	£
Sales revenue		17 800
Cost of sales		7 120
Gross profit		10 680
Less expenses		
Wages	3 420	
Rent	1 400	
Marketing	600	
Insurance	1 700	
	7 120	
Net profit		3 560

The values for gross profit (£10 680) minus total expenses (£7 120) will enable the business to calculate its net profit (£3 560).

Calculating net profit margin

From the statement of comprehensive income for Revision Ltd above, the net profit margin is calculated as follows:

$$\text{NPM} = \frac{\text{Net profit}}{\text{Sales revenue}} \times 100$$

$$= \frac{3 560}{17 800} \times 100$$

$$= 20\%$$

Interpreting the net profit margin

Revision Ltd has a net profit margin of 20 per cent. For every £ it makes in sales, it generates £0.20 in gross profit.

If the net profit margin falls, the enterprise may take steps to reduce its expenses or increase its sales revenue.

Now try this

Calculate the net margin profit of a company with sales revenue of £20 800 and a net profit of £5200.

 Use the formula for NPM.

Liquidity ratios

The current ratio and the liquid capital ratio measure the liquidity of an enterprise – its ability to be able to pay its short-term debts (current liabilities).

Current assets and liabilities

An enterprise's current assets must be *greater* than its current liabilities so that it is able to pay its bills.

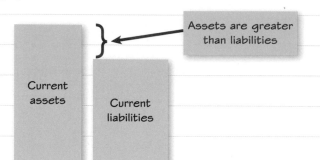

Paying liabilities

Current assets are made up of both cash and inventory (stock). An enterprise may have difficulty paying its liabilities if current assets are mainly in the form of inventory.

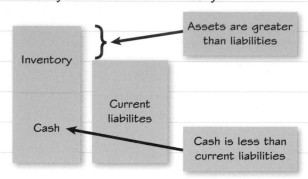

Current ratio and liquid capital ratio

To understand the liquidity of an enterprise two ratios are calculated – one which *includes* the inventory (stock) and another which *excludes* it.

Find the information

The information for these ratios is extracted from the statement of financial position.

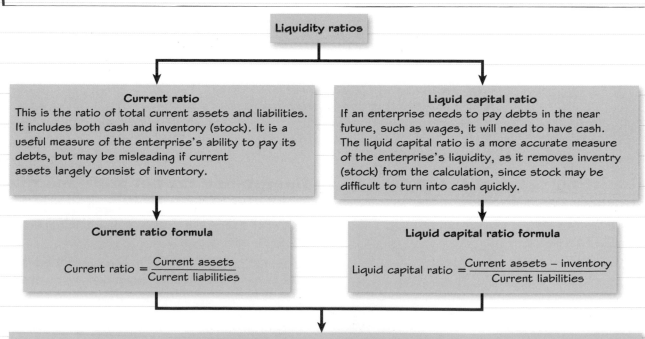

Liquidity ratios

Current ratio
This is the ratio of total current assets and liabilities. It includes both cash and inventory (stock). It is a useful measure of the enterprise's ability to pay its debts, but may be misleading if current assets largely consist of inventory.

Liquid capital ratio
If an enterprise needs to pay debts in the near future, such as wages, it will need to have cash. The liquid capital ratio is a more accurate measure of the enterprise's liquidity, as it removes inventry (stock) from the calculation, since stock may be difficult to turn into cash quickly.

Current ratio formula

$$\text{Current ratio} = \frac{\text{Current assets}}{\text{Current liabilities}}$$

Liquid capital ratio formula

$$\text{Liquid capital ratio} = \frac{\text{Current assets – inventory}}{\text{Current liabilities}}$$

Interpreting current and liquid capital ratios
Current assets must be higher than current liabilities. Most enterprises will accept 1.5:2.1 for the current ratio as it includes inventory. If either ratio falls below 1:1, the enterprise will struggle to pay its debts because it has insufficient cash. It would be advised to reduce the quantity of its inventory and increase its cash levels.

Now try this

An enterprise has current assets of £77 000 and short-term debts of £56 000. It has £22 000 of unsold inventory (stock). Calculate **(a)** its current ratio **(b)** its liquid capital ratio. Interpret your findings in each case.

 Make sure you use the right figures for each of the calculations.

Cash, sales and purchases

Cash is the liquid assets of the enterprise. It is mainly generated by **sales** and is used to make **purchases** in order for the business to operate.

Liquid assets

Cash is the money that an enterprise can access easily to pay its short-term liabilities. Liquid assets may consist of:

Money in the enterprise's bank account – its bank balance. This may include an overdraft and loans

Invoices (debtors) expected to be paid within a few days

Liquid assets

Notes and coins in the till

Products that can be sold easily

Importance of liquid assets

Liquidity is a measure of an enterprise's ability to convert its assets into cash. Cash is the most liquid asset. Revise liquidity on page 33.

Cash is a current asset

Revise current assets on page 26.

Sales

Sales of goods and services is the main source of cash for most enterprises.

Purchases

An enterprise needs cash to make purchases in order for the business to operate smoothly. Purchases may include:

- raw materials required to produce goods for sale
- expenses such as wages and salaries, heating and lighting, insurance and marketing
- business equipment such as machinery, office equipment and computers.

Now try this

Why are invoices still to be paid by an enterprise's customers viewed as less liquid than money held in the enterprise's bank account?

Remember that liquidity relates to how easy it is to convert an asset into cash.

Cash flow

Cash flow refers to the money coming into the enterprise each day – its **inflows** – and leaving the enterprise – its **outflows**. Depending on whether the enterprise has greater inflows or outflows of cash over a period of time, it will have either positive or negative liquidity.

Cash inflows and outflows

Payments from customers are cash inflows. When an enterprise pays a bill, this is an example of a cash outflow. The difference between outflows and inflows is the amount of cash in the enterprise – this is its **net cash flow**.

An enterprise needs to know how much cash is flowing in and out, and its net cash flow, so that it can ensure it has sufficient money to cover purchases and other running costs such as wages, rent and any monthly loan repayments.

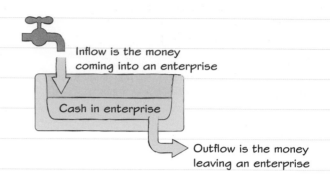

Inflow is the money coming into an enterprise

Cash in enterprise

Outflow is the money leaving an enterprise

Examples of cash inflows and outflows

INFLOWS
- Revenue from sales of goods and services
- Owner's capital
- Capital introduced, for example money from family and friends or from additional investors such as shareholders
- Bank loans
- Rent from property owned by enterprise
- Sale of assets

££££ → Enterprise → ££££

OUTFLOWS (purchases, including running costs)
- Raw materials for manufacture of goods
- Wages and salaries
- Heating, lighting and power
- Fuel for vans
- Rent
- Insurance and business rates
- Internet and phone charges
- Marketing
- Monthly loan repayments

Positive and negative liquidity

 An enterprise experiences **positive liquidity** If cash inflows over time are *greater* than cash outflows. It will have cash to pay for purchases.

An enterprise experiences **negative liquidity** if its cash inflows over time are *less* than its cash outflows. It will not have sufficient cash to pay for purchases.

Now try this

An enterprise had cash sales of £25 000 in May. In the same month, it spent £15 000 on raw materials. It began the month with £15 000 in its bank account. Rent, rates and other business expenses were £2000. Identify the cash inflows.

 Work out which of the figures are actually cash inflows and not cash outflows.

Cash flow forecasts

Enterprises collect cash flow data and use it to produce **cash flow statements** and **cash flow forecasts**. They use this information to monitor and control cash flow.

Cash flow statement

This records the enterprise's actual cash inflows and outflows over the previous 12 months. It is used by the enterprise to monitor the flow of cash.

Analysis of the previous year's cash flow statement may be used to produce the enterprise's cash flow forecast.

Cash flow forecast

This predicts the enterprise's likely cash inflows from sales, and outflows (purchases) each month over a period of time. The forecast allows the enterprise to calculate net cash flow and ensure it has sufficient cash to cover its running costs.

It is also used to determine net current asset requirements – the working capital needed to operate the business – and to make business decisions.

A cash flow forecast

Here is an extract from a cash flow forecast for Megan's sandwich delivery business covering the first quarter of the year (three months).

The total receipts row shows the **cash inflows** (sales) for each month. In January, total receipts
= £1000 + £250
= £1250

The total payments row shows the **cash outflows** (purchases) for each month. In January, total payments
= £750 + £200
   + £150 + £300
= £1400

This is a *negative* net cash flow (shown in brackets) where total payments are greater than total receipts.

Cash flow forecast for Megan's Sandwiches for January–March 2019

2019	January (£)	February (£)	March (£)
Cash inflows			
Sandwich sales	1000	2500	3000
Soft drinks	250	750	1000
Business loan			2000
Total receipts	**1250**	**3250**	**6000**
Cash outflows			
Bread and rolls	750	900	1120
Fillings	200	250	300
Soft drinks	150	225	400
Rent	300	300	300
Total payments	**1400**	**1675**	**2120**
Net inflow/outflow	**(150)**	**1575**	**3880**
Opening balance	**2500**	**2100**	**3675**
Closing balance	**2100**	**3675**	**7555**

The **net inflow/outflow** – the **net cash flow** – figure is calculated as total receipts (cash inflows) less total payments (cash outflows). In February, there is a net cash flow figure of £1575 (£3250 – £1675).

The closing balance at the end of the month is calculated by adding together the net cash flow and the opening balance.

The **closing balance** in one month is the money available to the enterprise at the end of the month. The closing balance is carried forward to the next month and becomes the **opening balance**. At the end of February, the closing balance was £3675. This was carried forward to become the opening balance in March.

How to calculate net cash flow and closing balance

Step 1:
Cash inflows (receipts) – Cash outflows (payment) = Net cash flow

Step 2:
Net cash flow + Opening balance = Closing balance

Now try this

Using the figures in the cash flow forecast, calculate the closing balance for April if total receipts were £3200 and total payments were £2350.

Remember to use the two-step process when calculating the closing balance.

Analysis of cash flow information

The differences between forecast and actual cash flow can alert an enterprise to cash flow problems. Cash flow information can be analysed to find out where there is a problem – in inflows or outflows. The size of the closing balance will indicate to the enterprise that it may need to take action to improve cash flow.

Analysing the cash flow for Colin's Bike Repair Shop

Here is an extract from a cash flow forecast for Colin's Bike Repair Shop covering February to April.

Cash flow forecast for Colin's Bike Repair Shop for February–April 2019

2019	January (£)	February (£)	March (£)
Cash inflows			
Repairs	2500	3000	3500
Spare part sales	950	1000	1300
Bank loan		2000	
Total receipts	3450	6000	4800
Cash outflows			
Cycle frames	1900	2120	2400
Bike chains	750	1900	2200
Tyres	225	800	1000
Rent	300	300	1000
Loan repayment			75
Total payments	3175	5120	6675
Net inflow/outflow	275	880	(1425)
Opening balance	500	775	1655
Closing balance	775	1655	230

Total receipts (cash inflows) show a large increase between February and March, mainly due to the £2000 bank loan.

Rent increased in April from £300 to £1000 per month. The enterprise may have moved to larger premises.

Monthly loan repayments start in April because the enterprise borrowed £2000 in March.

There is a negative net cash outflow in April of £1425. A move to larger premises (the big increase in rent) may mean the enterprise needs additional inventory (stock). Colin must ensure that cash inflows in future months increase, otherwise the business may face financial difficulties.

The closing balance forecast for April is only £230 as a result of the impact of the net cash outflow. If there is another cash outflow in May, Colin will need to take steps to improve cash flow.

Positive closing balance

👍 **Large positive closing balance** – the enterprise has plenty of cash. It can pay its bills, and there will be money for expansion plans or to invest.

👍 **Small positive closing balance** – the enterprise has cash to pay its bills, and to trade. It may not have enough money to purchase new fixed assets.

Negative closing balance

👎 **Small negative closing balance** – the enterprise does not have cash to pay its bills. It may be able to get a short-term bank loan or overdraft to enable it to continue trading while it takes action to sort out its cash flow problem.

👎 **Large negative closing balance** – the enterprise does not have cash to pay its bills. It will have to take immediate action to improve its inflows and reduce its outflows, otherwise it may cease trading.

Now try this

If the figures in Colin's cash flow forecast for May showed a cash inflow of £6000 and a cash outflow of £6400, what would be the closing balance for May?

Remember to take into account the opening balance.

Cash flow problems and forecasting

Cash flow problems arise when the enterprise has to pay out more money than it has coming in each month. There may be several reasons for this. Cash flow forecasting is essential to the health of an enterprise.

Why can cash flow problems happen?

An enterprise that does not produce cash flow statements or forecasts will not be able to monitor its actual and forecast cash inflows and outflows each month. It may not be aware when cash flow problems arise

The enterprise may try to grow too quickly. For example, it may have ambitious sales targets, but not have enough cash to buy the raw materials required to make all the products customers have ordered

Poor cash flow management. This may arise from poor record keeping, such as:
- the enterprise may not record when invoices are due for payment, and therefore not know to chase customers (debtors) who are slow to pay
- the cash flow forecast may contain errors

Causes of cash flow problems

Some debtors (customers) may take longer to pay than the terms given on the invoice (trade credit) or may not pay at all (known as bad debt)

The enterprise may receive several bills all at once, resulting in more money going out than coming in. This could include requests from customers for refunds for faulty or unwanted goods

The enterprise may have to pay unexpected bills, such as for the repair of faulty equipment

Benefits of cash flow forecasting

 Timing of cash inflows and outflows is known.

 Potential problems can be spotted quickly.

 The purchase of expensive items can be planned to suit cash flow.

 The enterprise can plan when to expand or reduce its activities depending on cash flow.

Risks of not forecasting cash flow

👎 Late inflows (debtors) can be identified.

👎 There may not be enough cash to pay employees, suppliers and running costs.

👎 Suppliers may refuse to trade with an enterprise that does not pay on time.

👎 The enterprise may need an expensive loan or overdraft to cover short-term cash flow problems.

👎 The enterprise may run out of money and have to cease trading.

Now try this

Explain how over-ambitious sales targets can impact on the cash flow statement.

 Remember that the cash flow statement shows the actual inflows and outflows of cash in a specific period of time.

Improving cash flow

Once an enterprise has spotted a potential cash flow problem, it will need to take action to change the timing or amount of cash inflows and outflows.

Ways to improve timing of cash flows

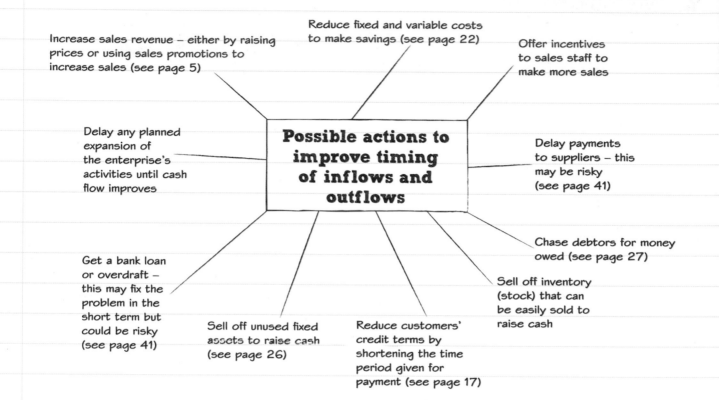

Increase sales revenue – either by raising prices or using sales promotions to increase sales (see page 5)

Reduce fixed and variable costs to make savings (see page 22)

Offer incentives to sales staff to make more sales

Delay any planned expansion of the enterprise's activities until cash flow improves

Possible actions to improve timing of inflows and outflows

Delay payments to suppliers – this may be risky (see page 41)

Chase debtors for money owed (see page 27)

Get a bank loan or overdraft – this may fix the problem in the short term but could be risky (see page 41)

Sell off unused fixed assets to raise cash (see page 26)

Reduce customers' credit terms by shortening the time period given for payment (see page 17)

Sell off inventory (stock) that can be easily sold to raise cash

Potential impacts of improving cash flow

The measures taken to improve cash flow can themselves create difficulties for the business:

👎 **Reducing customers' credit terms** may result in fewer sales if customers switch to other businesses that offer more favourable credit terms.

👎 **Selling off inventory** could be at a lower cost than the purchase cost, resulting in a financial loss.

👎 **Selling off unused fixed assets** such as machinery or company cars may mean that the enterprise is willing to accept a lower price for these assets than they are worth.

👎 **Delaying planned expansion** could mean that the enterprise is not able to take advantage of business opportunities.

👎 **Reducing costs** by purchasing cheaper supplies or laying off part of the workforce could result in poorer quality products and dissatisfied customers.

Now try this

Explain how the timings of cash inflows can impact upon an enterprise's cash flow.

 Remember that an enterprise will have to pay some of its running costs on a monthly basis.

Break-even

Break-even is when revenue from sales and costs are the same. There is no profit and no loss. At this point, the money that the enterprise has made selling a product is equal to the cost of making the product. The break-even point can be calculated using a formula.

Loss, break-even and profit

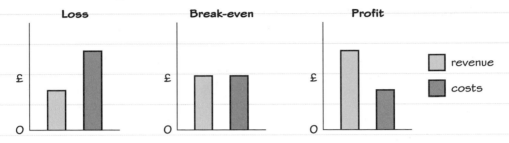

Loss   Break-even   Profit   ☐ revenue ☐ costs

Calculating break-even

To calculate break-even, you need to know the following information:

1 sales price per unit

2 variable cost per unit

3 fixed costs.

Costs and sales

To understand break-even, it may help you to revise:

- costs (variable, fixed and total)
- sales (total revenue).

(See pages 21 and 22.)

Break-even point

The break-even point is the number of units an enterprise will need to produce and sell in order to cover its costs. One unit fewer means the enterprise will make a loss, one more unit means it will make a profit.

Break-even formula

A formula can be used to calculate the break-even point:

$$\text{Break-even point} = \frac{\text{Fixed costs}}{\text{Sales price per unit} - \text{Variable cost per unit}}$$

Case study

Gamma Garments Ltd manufactures designer dresses, which it sells for £200 each. Its fixed costs are £100 000 and its variable costs are £40 per dress. It must sell 625 dresses to break even, as shown below:

This figure (160) will **fall** if the selling price is **reduced** or variable costs **increase**.

This figure (160) will **increase** if the selling price **increase** or variable costs **fall**.

$$\frac{100\,000}{200 - 40}$$

$$= \frac{100\,000}{160}$$

$$= \textbf{625 dresses}$$

This means the break-even point will **increase** and the business will have to sell more dresses before it starts to make a profit.

This means the break-even point will **fall** and the business will start to make a profit at a lower level of sales.

Now try this

Niki makes gold earrings. The sales price of each pair of earrings is £80. The variable cost of each pair is £20. Fixed costs are £5400. Using the break-even formula, calculate:

(a) Niki's break-even point.

(b) the new break-even point if the price of a pair of earrings is raised to £110 and the costs remain the same.

This is the number of pairs of earrings Niki will need to sell in order not to make a loss.

Break-even charts

A break-even chart can be drawn to show how many products an enterprise needs to sell in order to break-even. This is marked on the chart as the break-even point.

Information for break-even chart

Before drawing a break-even chart, you will need the following information about the product:

- fixed costs
- variable costs
- total revenue (sales)
- selling price per unit.

How to draw a break-even chart

1. Draw the **fixed costs** line.

2. Draw the **total costs** line (variable + fixed costs).

3. Draw the **total revenue** line.

4. Mark on the **break-even** point – where total costs and total revenue lines cross.

An example of a break-even chart

Total revenue – this red line starts at zero as no sales means no income coming in for the enterprise. To work out the total revenue, multiply any unit of output by the price per unit.

This green line shows the total costs (fixed costs + variable costs) at each level of output. The total costs line starts at £4000 on the vertical axis, showing that even if nothing is produced the business will still have to pay its fixed costs of £4000.

The vertical axis on the chart shows costs and revenue (sales) in £.

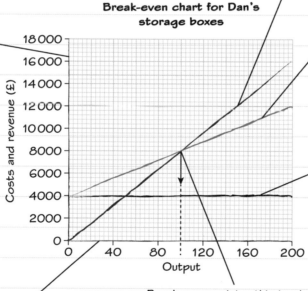

Break-even chart for Dan's storage boxes

Fixed costs – this is shown as a horizontal blue line on the chart as fixed costs do not change with output. Dan's storage boxes have fixed costs of £4000.

The horizontal axis shows the quantity of boxes (output/sales).

Break-even point – this is where the total costs and total revenue lines cross. Dan has to produce 100 boxes to break-even.

Label the chart

Remember to:

- give the chart a title
- label the axes, lines and break-even point.

Now try this

Give **two** items of information an enterprise needs to know before it can construct a break-even chart.

 Think about the information contained in a break-even chart.

Interpreting a break-even chart

A break-even chart provides lots of financial information about a product. It shows the number of units required to make the enterprise a profit (or a loss). It can be used to identify the margin of safety.

Profit or loss

When the total revenue line is higher than total costs line, the enterprise makes a profit. When it is lower, it makes a loss.

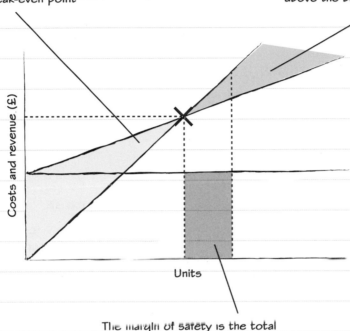

Loss is shown by the space between costs and revenue below the break-even point

Profit is shown by the space between costs and revenue above the break-even point

Costs and revenue (£)

Units

The margin of safety is the total number of sales that can be lost before the enterprise loses money.
Margin of safety = Sales − Break-even point

Analysing the information in a break-even chart

By analysing a break-even chart we can calculate the following:
- The level of output at which total costs equals total revenue (the break-even point).
- The total fixed costs, which will be the same at any level of output or sales.
- The total variable costs at any level of output or sales (total costs minus fixed costs).
- The total costs at any level of output or sales (fixed costs plus variable costs).
- The margin of safety (planned sales minus break-even point).
- The level of profit or loss made at an level of output or sales (total costs minus total revenue).

Now try this

Explain why it is important for an enterprise to set a margin of safety.

Consider the impact on the enterprise if sales fall.

Using break-even analysis in planning

Enterprises use break-even analysis as a planning tool to enable them to consider the impact of different levels of output, sales and prices on the break-even point.

Costs

👊 **Costs increase** – break-even point rises. The enterprise makes less profit. *Action to take:* The enterprise may need to sell more items to break-even. It may try to reduce costs. It may raise the selling price.

👍 **Costs fall** – lowers break-even point. The enterprise makes more profit. The lower the break-even point, the fewer sales are required to break-even.

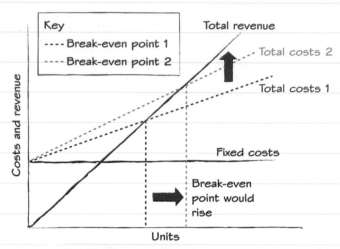

When costs increase, the break-even point increases.

Selling price

👍 **Increase in selling price** – break-even point lowers. Fewer sales required to break-even.

👊 **Decrease in selling price** – break-even point rises. *Action to take:* The enterprise will need to make more sales to break even or reduce its variable costs.

Sales (revenue)

👍 **Sales increase** – lowers break-even point. The margin of safety increases Revenue increases and the enterprise makes more profit.

👊 **Sales fall** – break-even point rises. The margin of safety decreases. *Action to take:* The enterprise may try to improve sales by lowering the selling price. This increases the number of goods needed to be sold to break-even. It may also reduce its variable costs.

Increasing the selling price

A change in the selling price can have the opposite effect to the one hoped for by the enterprise – to lower the break-even point. Customers may not be prepared to pay the increased price and switch to a rival, cheaper brand.

Falling sales

An enterprise may lower the price for a short time only to boost sales and attract new customers.

Now try this

Ushma and Raj run a restaurant. The enterprise is only just breaking even. Their energy charges have increased, and they are considering raising their prices.

1 How will this affect the break-even point?

2 Identify **one** risk associated with increasing prices.

When an enterprise is just breaking even it will not be making much profit.

Had a look ☐   Nearly there ☐   Nailed it! ☐

Limitations of break-even analysis

Break-even analysis is a useful planning tool, with many benefits. There may be risks involved in not using break-even analysis, but it also has limitations.

Benefits of break-even analysis

 Fixed and variable costs are known.

 Potential sales revenue can be calculated.

 The number of items needed to be sold in order to make a profit is known.

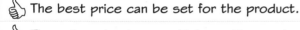 The enterprise can take action to increase profit, for example by reducing costs.

 The best price can be set for the product.

 The enterprise knows which are the most profitable products to make.

The margin of safety is known.

Risks of not using break-even analysis

Costs are unknown so action cannot be taken to reduce them if they are too high. For example, if inventory (stock) is sold below cost price, the enterprise will make a loss.

The enterprise will not know how many items need to be sold in order to make a profit. If it sells too few, it may make a loss.

Setting the price of products may be guesswork, resulting in too high or too low a price.

The margin of safety is not known.

Limitations

Break-even analysis makes a number of assumptions. Sometimes these may not be accurate.

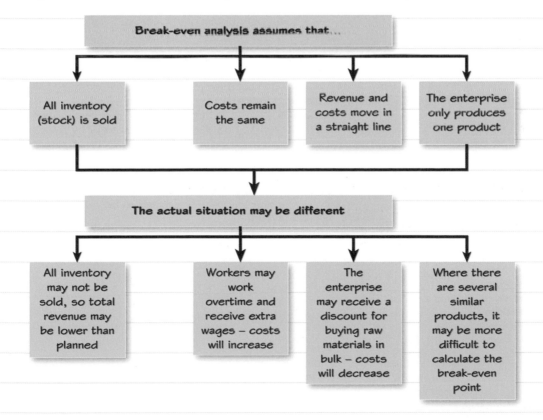

Break-even analysis assumes that...

| All inventory (stock) is sold | Costs remain the same | Revenue and costs move in a straight line | The enterprise only produces one product |

The actual situation may be different

| All inventory may not be sold, so total revenue may be lower than planned | Workers may work overtime and receive extra wages – costs will increase | The enterprise may receive a discount for buying raw materials in bulk – costs will decrease | Where there are several similar products, it may be more difficult to calculate the break-even point |

Now try this

An enterprise manufactures office furniture with raw materials imported from India. It also purchases components supplied by a local firm. Most of its workforce is paid an hourly rate based upon the living wage, which is set by the government. What factors could impact on the enterprise's break-even point?

 Consider the impact of changes in variable costs on the break-even point.

The need for business finance

Business finance is required for different purposes at every stage of an enterprise's activities – from start-up to expansion.

Different business stages and finance required

Start-up enterprise	→	Established enterprise	→	Expanding enterprise

Purpose of finance
To set up the enterprise, the owner may require finance to obtain equipment, hire workers, rent or buy premises and purchase inventory (stock).

Purpose of finance
An enterprise that is generating some profits may require finance to ensure it is able to pay its short-term liabilities and stay solvent.

Purpose of finance
A well-established enterprise may have plans to grow the business, for example, to produce and sell more products, introduce new products, enter a new market, or open a new branch. The enterprise may require finance to support its expansion plans, for example to obtain new machinery or premises.

Key questions an enterprise needs to ask when it is considering whether to obtain business finance

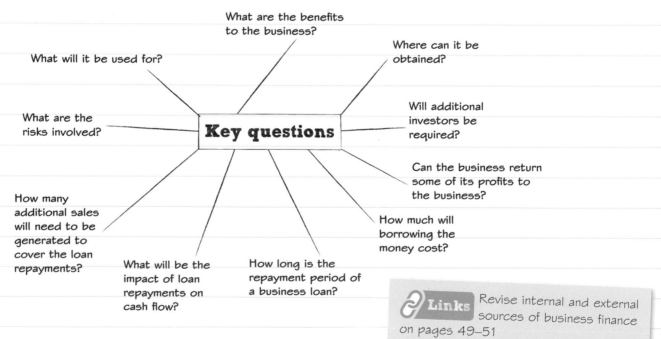

What are the benefits to the business?

What will it be used for?

Where can it be obtained?

What are the risks involved?

Key questions

Will additional investors be required?

Can the business return some of its profits to the business?

How many additional sales will need to be generated to cover the loan repayments?

What will be the impact of loan repayments on cash flow?

How long is the repayment period of a business loan?

How much will borrowing the money cost?

Links Revise internal and external sources of business finance on pages 49–51

Now try this

Why is it sometimes difficult for a person to obtain start-up finance from a bank?

 Think about the business risks associated with new business ideas.

Internal sources of finance

When an enterprise requires money, depending on the purpose, it may be able to provide the finance itself. Internal sources of finance each have benefits and disadvantages.

Owner funds

Most new owners supply most of the start-up capital themselves because profits have yet to be made.

👍 No interest is payable.

👍 If the enterprise is successful, the owner may in time get back their investment with a profit.

👎 The owner may not have sufficient savings to invest in the enterprise.

👎 If the enterprise fails, the owner may lose their investment.

Retained profits

These can used to finance the growth of the enterprise (see page 25).

👍 Money does not have to be repaid and no interest is payable.

👎 New enterprises will not be at the stage to have retained profits.

👎 Many enterprises may not make sufficient profits to be able to invest them back into the business.

Sale of assets

Vehicles, premises owned by the enterprise, machinery and equipment can be sold to give the enterprise cash to pay short-term liabilities, to address cash flow problems or to reinvest in the enterprise (see page 26).

👍 A good way to raise money from assets that are no longer needed.

👍 It may avoid the need for a loan.

👎 Some enterprises may have not have assets that they can sell. It may take time to sell larger assets.

Net current assets

This is money that is immediately available to the enterprise – its working capital. It may use this to pay short-term liabilities such as money owed to suppliers (see pages 26 and 28).

👍 A quick way to raise money.

👎 If selling off inventory (stock), the enterprise may have to accept a lower selling price.

This firm needed to sell its premises when it encountered a cash-flow problem.

Now try this

Over the last three years, a manufacturing enterprise has retained 20 per cent of its profits. Explain why it may have chosen to do this.

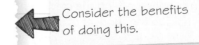 Consider the benefits of doing this.

49

External sources of finance – short term

If an enterprise does not have sufficient internal sources of finance to fund its activities, it may seek finance from external sources. Some external sources of finance are short term – used mainly to improve cash flow and ensure the enterprise has sufficient money to pay its short-term liabilities. On this page, you will revise short-term external sources of finance, their benefits and disadvantages.

Bank overdrafts

The bank allows the enterprise to spend more than it has in its bank balance up to an agreed limit. This is a type of loan, and may be used by start-ups and small businesses.

👍 A flexible method of finance as the enterprise only uses the overdraft facility when it needs to, for example to meet a cash flow problem.

👍 Can be arranged quickly.

👎 Interest, which may be at a high rate, and charges are payable to the bank.

👎 Has to be repaid within a short amount of time.

Credit cards

A common method of finance used by large and small enterprises. It can be used to purchase stock and finance business trips and pay hotel bills (see page 19).

👍 Instant source of finance.

👍 Allows purchases to be made on behalf of the enterprise.

👎 Interest rate can be high if the amount is not paid back within the interest-free period.

👎 Only suitable for purchases up to an agreed credit limit.

Trade credit

Current assets are purchased on credit with payment terms of 30–90 days. Trade credit is often used by enterprises to buy raw materials or products to sell on (see page 17).

👍 Good for cash flow (see page 38). In some cases, the enterprise may be able to sell on the products before paying the supplier for them.

👍 No interest is paid.

👎 Can only be used to buy certain types of goods.

👎 Loan is only available up to the payment terms agreed with the supplier.

Now try this

Why do suppliers offer trade credit terms to their business customers? What are the risks to the supplier of offering trade credit?

Consider the potential impact on sales revenue and cash flow.

External sources of finance – long term

External sources of finance may be used to obtain expensive non-current assets and support business growth. This type of finance is usually repaid over a long period of time.

Bank loans

This is money borrowed by the enterprise at an agreed rate of interest. It is paid back over a period of time, for example 3, 5 or 10 years. Bank loans may be used to purchase non-current assets such as vehicles, machinery or property.

👍 The interest rate on the loan is fixed during the repayment period even if general interest rates increase.

👍 Enterprises can budget more easily as it is a fixed cost.

👍 The rate of interest is usually lower than an overdraft.

👎 Interest rates may be high and the bank may want security on the loan.

👎 Failure to repay the loan may lead to the enterprise becoming bankrupt.

Government grants

Local and national government grants are used to develop the economy. They may be given to certain enterprises, for example to enable them to create jobs in a certain area.

👍 Grants do not need to be paid back.

👎 Only certain enterprises are able to obtain government grants.

Peer-to-peer lending

Small investors invest in an enterprise, usually a start-up, in exchange for a return on their investment.

👍 It may be used by enterprises that may have difficulty getting traditional forms of finance, such as a bank loan.

👎 Interest payments may be higher than traditional types of finance.

Hire purchase

This allows the enterprise to purchase an asset such as equipment or machinery by paying a deposit followed by regular monthly instalments (an agreed sum of money) over a period of time.

👍 Once the enterprise has paid all the instalments, it owns the asset.

👎 It is a more expensive method of purchase than buying the asset with cash at the outset.

Leasing

This allows an enterprise to have use of the asset, such as an expensive item of equipment or machinery, over a period of time without buying it. The owner of the asset lends it to the enterprise for regular payments.

👍 The enterprise can have modern equipment without having to pay out a large amount to buy it.

👍 The enterprise has the asset it requires for the time it needs it. It is not left with an unwanted asset at the end of the leasing period.

👎 The enterprise does not own the asset. It returns the equipment to the owner at the end of the leasing period.

Venture capital

These are funds from a professional investor (venture capitalist) who expects a return on their investment and a share of the ownership of the enterprise.

👍 The enterprise may benefit from the expert guidance of the venture capitalist.

👎 The venture capitalist may want to be involved in decision making, and the enterprise owner may lose some management control.

Now try this

Suggest an appropriate external source of finance that could be used:

(a) to pay for supplies

(b) to obtain an expensive piece of equipment that requires regular updating

(c) to finance the production of a new product

(d) to finance research into a new environmentally friendly product.

Consider the specific features and characteristics in each case.

Your Component 3 set task

Component 3 will be assessed through a task, which will be set by Pearson. In this assessed task you will be provided with a case study of a small to medium enterprise (SME), and a series of activities to complete.

Revising your skills

Your assessed task could cover any of the essential content in the component. You can revise the component content in this Revision Guide. This skills section is designed to **revise skills** that might be needed in your assessed task. The section uses selected content and outcomes to provide examples of ways of applying your skills.

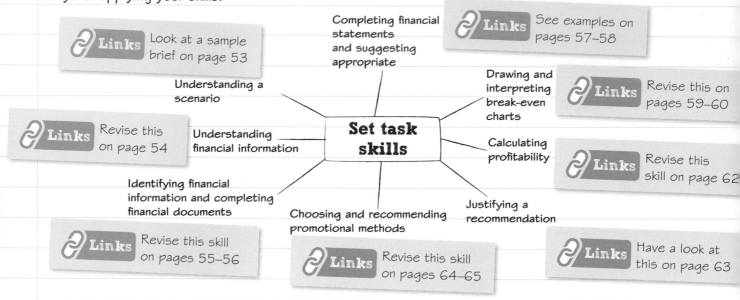

Links Look at a sample brief on page 53

Links See examples on pages 57–58

Completing financial statements and suggesting appropriate

Understanding a scenario

Links Revise this on pages 59–60

Drawing and interpreting break-even charts

Links Revise this on page 54

Understanding financial information

Set task skills

Calculating profitability

Links Revise this skill on page 62

Identifying financial information and completing financial documents

Choosing and recommending promotional methods

Justifying a recommendation

Links Revise this skill on pages 55–56

Links Revise this skill on pages 64–65

Links Have a look at this on page 63

Workflow

The process might follow these steps as you identify and use an appropriate selection of skills and knowledge to:

- ☑ read and understand a scenario
- ☑ complete financial documents, such as an invoice
- ☑ prepare financial statements
- ☑ interpret financial statements
- ☑ perform calculations using business data
- ☑ suggest appropriate promotional activities for a given enterprise or product
- ☑ justify/choose/recommend an appropriate action.

Check the Pearson website

The activities and sample response extracts in this section are provided to help you to revise content and skills. Ask your teacher or check the Pearson website for the latest **Sample Assessment Material** and **Mark Scheme** to get an indication of the structure of the actual assessed task and what this requires of you. The details of the actual assessed task may change so always make sure you are up to date.

Now try this

Visit the Pearson website and find the page containing the course materials for the BTEC Tech Award in Enterprise. Look at the latest Component 3 Sample Assessment Material for an indication of:

- the structure of your assessment
- how much time you are allowed
- what scenario and information might be provided to you
- the activities you are required to answer and how to format your responses
- whether you can take a calculator into the task.

Understanding a scenario

When reading a scenario about an enterprise, make sure you understand it before completing any activities. All activities will be based on the scenario and relate to promotion and finance for the enterprise. Additional information may be given in some activities to help you to complete the tasks.

Scenario

The scenario given below is used as an example to show the skills you will need. The content of a scenario will be different each year and the format may be different. The details of the actual assessed task may change so always make sure you are up to date.

Features in a scenario

When reading a scenario and any additional information, you may find some of the following features:

- Product features
- Unique or special product features
- Target market
- Promotional activities
- Costs
- Revenue streams
- Plans for the future.

Creating Together

Stella is a young fashion designer. After completing her college course, she travelled to India where she met Ida, who makes bags using locally produced cloth. Stella and Ida formed an enterprise, Creating Together, which produces stylish cloth bags that are sold in UK supermarkets.

They now want to design and produce a range of clothing aimed at 16–21-year olds, and have appointed you as their promotion and finance assistant to help them.

It can be useful to underline key features in the scenario to help you focus on them.

Make sure you understand the background of the business.

Identify any special features of its products and start to think about the influence of these features on aspects such as cost and promotional choices.

Become familiar with its plans for the future.

Start thinking about potential promotional activities in the promotional mix. Consider the type of promotion that will appeal to this age group, for example social media and fashion magazines.

Links To revise the promotional mix, see pages 1–13.

Now try this

Why is it important for Creating Together to identify a target market for its new product range?

Consider both the promotional mix and the costs of promotion.

Links To revise targeting and segmenting markets, see pages 9 and 10.

Understanding financial information

You will need to interpret financial information and show that you understand the processes involved in finance and promotion for an enterprise.

Stella and Ida have started to draw a diagram to show the flow of financial documents. The diagram shows the order in which documents are sent and received when a customer buys cloth bags from Creating Together. Each arrow shows who sends the document and who receives it.

Financial documents

You could be asked to complete any of the financial documents used in the buying and

 **Links** Revise financial documents on pages 14–18.

selling process. Revise their purpose, the order in which they are sent, who sends each document and who receives it.

The examples in this section use selected financial documents to help you revise. Ask your teacher or check the Sample Assessment Material and Mark Scheme on the Pearson website for details of your actual assessment. Assessment details may change so always make sure you are up to date.

1 The start of the process requires the customer to prepare a document which tells the supplier the products it requires. The student has correctly labelled this as a purchase order.

2 The student has correctly labelled this as a delivery note. This document provides details of the goods sent by the supplier (Creating Together) to the customer.

3 Sometimes goods are returned to the supplier by the customer after they have been paid and the value of these goods needs to be taken into account when the customer next orders some goods. The student has correctly identified that a credit note ensures this happens.

Complete the rest of the diagram showing the order of documents sent and received: purchase order; delivery note; credit note. In each blank box write one of these documents and draw the direction arrow.

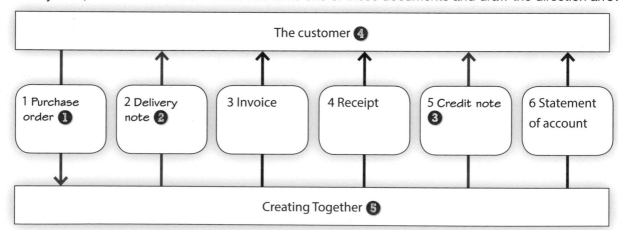

4 In this example, the *customer* could be a supermarket. At other times, the supermarket may be the *supplier*, for example when it sells goods online.

5 In this example, Creating Together is the *supplier*. At other times, it may be the *customer*, for example when buying cloth from its suppliers.

Which document would be prepared by the supplier stating the amount of money paid by the customer for the products they have received?

The customer needs to have proof that they are paying for products they have received.

Had a look ☐   Nearly there ☐   Nailed it! ☐

Identifying financial information

You may need to identify financial information and use it to complete financial documents.

Look carefully at the details of the products to be supplied. You will need to record them accurately when completing the invoice. This is particularly important where products look similar – in this case, rucksacks. Make sure you record the correct catalogue number.

Creating Together needs to send an invoice to a customer, Value Supermarkets plc. This is an extract from the customer's purchase order.

Purchase Order		Purchase order number: 234/56			
Value Supermarkets plc Midtown EB6 7ZZ					
Item description	Catalogue No.	Price per item		Quantity	Total price
		£	p		£	p
Logo bags	345/T	8	00	100		
Small yellow rucksacks	674/SY	4	00	20		
Large blue rucksacks	674/LB	4	50	20		

You may be given financial information in order to complete a financial document. All the information you need will be there.

Look carefully at the sample invoice on page 56 to see what information is required. Now look at how the student has carefully underlined the information in the sample purchase order. Underlining, circling or highlighting information will make it easier to transfer the correct information to the form.

Sometimes a *catalogue number* may be replaced by a *stock number* or, in the case of components for manufactured goods, *part number*. In all cases, the number will be *unique* to a particular product or part.

Completing an invoice from a purchase order

Step 1:
Look carefully at the financial document to be completed, such as the sample invoice on page 56. What information is required? Underline, circle or highlight the information you need to complete the form, as shown in the sample purchase order above.

Step 2:
Fill in the form with the information from the purchase order. This may include the catalogue or stock number, description of items, quantity ordered and price per item.

Step 3:
Make the following calculations:
1 Calculate the discount.
2 Calculate the VAT.
3 Calculate the total to pay.

The completed sample invoice and calculations are shown on page 56.

You will be given a blank form to complete.

The information to be included in an invoice may come from a number of sources, such as a purchase order, sales catalogue or delivery note.

Now try this

Why is it important to include the catalogue number or stock number of each item when preparing an invoice?

A catalogue or stock number is unique to each product.

Completing a financial document

You may need to complete financial documents using the information provided. You will be given a blank form to complete.

Stella and Ida have left you this email about the invoice.

> Hi
>
> Please prepare an invoice for the logo bags and rucksacks we delivered to Value Supermarkets plc last Tuesday. The invoice number is VS/78654/TV.
>
> Thanks.

Complete the invoice.

Financial documents

You might be asked to complete other financial documents in your actual assessment. Make sure you've revised all of them.

The sample email and invoice relate to financial information in the sample purchase order on page 55. To complete the invoice, you would need to select the financial information given in the purchase order.

Most invoices will require you to multiply (Number of items × Price), add up (total price of all items), work out percentages (discounts and VAT) and subtract (total cost of all items less discount). Here the student has correctly calculated the discount:

$$\frac{5}{100} \times £970 = £48.50$$

Sample response extract

INVOICE

INVOICE No: VS/78654/TV   **Date:** 30 November 2018

To: Value Supermarkets plc

Midtown EB6 7ZZ

Catalogue No	Description	Quantity	Price per item £	Price per item p	Total cost £	Total cost p
345/T	Logo bags	100	8	00	800	00
674/SY	Small yellow rucksacks	20	4	00	80	00
674/LB	Large blue rucksacks	20	4	50	90	00
				Total	970	00
				Discount @ 5%	48	50
				Total excluding VAT	921	50
				VAT @ 20%		
				Total to pay		

Financial documents must be completed in the correct order. Once you've checked that you have filled in the information correctly, then do the calculations. The total here is correct because it includes the full price of all the items.

The discount of £48.50 has been subtracted from the total of £970.

Discounts are calculated *after* you have calculated the full value of all goods supplied.

Value added tax (VAT) is added to the invoice after discounts have been deducted.

Check that you have written down the correct quantity of items and the price per item. If any details are filled in incorrectly, the total price will be wrong.

Now try this

Complete the invoice to be sent to Value Supermarkets plc.

$VAT = \frac{20}{100} \times$ Total excluding VAT. You could also use a calculator to work out the VAT.

Completing a statement of financial position

If you are asked to complete a statement of financial position, you will be given information and a statement to fill in.

🔗 **Links** To revise the statement of financial position, see pages 31–32.

Hi

I've worked with Ida to draw up a list of Creating Together's assets and liabilities. Here are the figures:

Computer	£1500	Debtors	£1500	3-year bank loan	£3000
Delivery van	£4000	Cash in bank	£1000	Owners'capita	£6000
Printing machine	£2000	Creditors	£4000		
Inventory	£4000	Overdraft	£1000		

Can you draw up a statement of financial position?

Thanks, Stella

Complete the form.

Before preparing the statement of financial position, make a note of which of the items are current assets, fixed assets, current liabilities and longterm liabilities.

Sample response extract

This is a good answer because the student has correctly identified the different categories of assets and liabilities, put them in the right order and completed the statement correctly.

Double-check that you've entered all the assets and liabilities.

Statement of financial position as of 31 December 2018

	£	£
Fixed assets		
Computer	1500	
Delivery van	4000	
Printing machine	2000	
		7500
Current assets		
Inventory	4000	
Debtors	1500	
Cash in bank	1000	
		6500
Total assets		14000
Current liabilities		
Creditors	4000	
Overdraft	1000	
		5000
Long-term liabilities		
Bank loan	3000	3000
Total liabilities		8000
Financed by		
Owners' capital		6000

The right-hand column contains the *total* of the various categories. In this case the enterprise has a total of £14000 in assets. (£7500 fixed assets + £6500 current assets)

Double-check that all the totals in the right-hand column are correct. For example, total liabilities are £8000 (£5000 current liabilities and £3000 non-current liabilities)

Now try this

An enterprise's total assets are £15500, the owner's capital is £8000 and its current liabilities are £1500. Calculate the value of its long-term liabilities.

Having prepared a statement of financial position, check:
Total assets = Total liabilities + Owner's capital

Suggesting appropriate actions

You may be asked to suggest appropriate actions for a financial statement you have completed.

Stella and Ida have decided to sell their 16–21 clothing range directly to consumers. They plan to offer customers credit over six months if they spend more than £200.

Explain how Creating Together's statement of financial position could be affected by this promotion.

Formula for gross profit margin

If you complete a statement of financial position or a statement of comprehensive income, you may be asked to suggest appropriate actions. For example:

- Explain how the use of promotional methods could have an impact on an enterprise's profit.
- Suggest how a promotion can be used to increase net profit.
- Explain how a promotion might affect the business's liquidity.

Sample response extract

The promotion will increase Creating Together's assets because there will be an increase in debtors. However, if some of its customers do not pay for all of the goods they have purchased within the six-month period (or don't pay at all), then the enterprise could experience liquidity problems and not be able to meet its shortterm current liabilities. This could be made worse if the business takes on additional creditors (liabilities) as a result of purchasing more materials on short-term credit to cover the increased output.

This is a good answer because the student has shown an understanding of how offering credit increases debtors, but also impacts upon liquidity. The point made about the increase in creditors is also important because the student links it with the potential liquidity problem that the enterprise might face.

You have discussed with Stella and Ida the potential risks of their promotional strategy. Suggest how the promotion could be made less risky.

Sample response extract

They could reduce the credit period from six months to three months, and only offer credit up to a maximum of £100 of purchases.

This is a good response because the student has chosen the two elements of the credit terms available to customers (amount of credit and length of credit).

Now try this

What are the advantages for Creating Together of offering two T-shirts for the price of one?

Consider both financial and non-financial advantages.

Drawing a break-even chart

You may be given some figures and asked to draw a break-even chart.

Links To revise how to draw a break-even chart, see page 44

Stella is looking at the costs and sales forecast for T-shirts. She has given you some costs and pricing information to use when drawing a break-even chart.

Forecasts	
Variable cost of a T-shirt	£5
Fixed costs	£2 000
Sales price of a T-shirt	£10

She plans to sell 700 T-shirts.

Draw a break-even chart for the T-shirts on the graph supplied.

You may find it helpful to complete the activity table before you start the chart.

Sample response extract

Activity table

No of T-shirts	0	300	800
Sales revenue	O	£3 000	£8 000
Variable costs	O		£4 000
Fixed costs	£2 000	£2 000	£2 000
Total costs	£2 000		

Variable costs = No. of T-shirts produced x £5

So the variable cost of 300 T-shirts would be:

300 x £5 = £1500

Total costs = Fixed costs + variable costs

Once you have calculated the variable cost of 300 T-shirts you will be able to calculate the total costs:

£2000 + £1500 = £3500

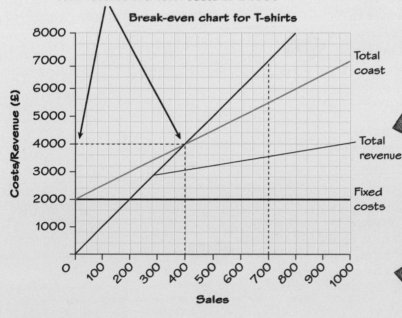

The break-even point is 400 T-shirts with total revenue and total costs at £4000

This is a good answer because the:

1 axes are correctly labelled.

2 different costs (total costs and fixed costs) have been correctly plotted and labelled

3 break-even point is correct (400 T-shirts with total revenue and total revenue both at £4000).

Planned sales of 700 T-shirts are above the break-even point so the business will be making a profit.

- -

Now try this

Calculate how much profit the enterprise will make if it sells 700 T-shirts.

Total revenue = Sales × Price

Total costs = Fixed costs + Variable costs

Interpreting break-even charts

Once you have drawn your break-even chart, you may need to explain how a change in the price of a product will change the position of the break-even point and the impact this may have on the margin of safety. You will also need to show that you understand how the use of a promotional method will impact on your break-even calculations.

 Links To revise interpretation of break-even charts, see page 45.

Stella and Ida decide that they will aim to sell 700 T-shirts.

Why is it important for them to know the margin of safety at this level of sales?

From the break-even chart on page 59, you have calculated that break-even output is 400 T-shirts.

Sample response extract

Knowing the margin of safety is important because it tells Stella and Ida the number of sales the enterprise can lose before it stops being profitable.

This is a good answer because the student has clearly shown that they understand what is meant by the margin of safety and its value to the owners of the enterprise.

After carrying out some research on their competitors, Stella and Ida have decided that they should reduce the price of T-shirts from £10 to £7.

How would reducing the price impact upon the break-even point, and why?

This is a good response because the student has correctly identified that the break-even point would increase and the reason why it would increase.

Sample response extract

The price decrease would increase the break-even point. In other words, they would have to sell more T-shirts before they start to make a profit. The reason for this is that it will take more sales in order to cover the fixed costs.

Remember that changes in price alter the *slope* of the total revenue line in the chart.

Outline one impact that reducing the price of the T-shirts will have on the enterprise's margin of safety.

Sample response extract

Lowering the price of the T-shirts will increase the break-even point and, as a result, the business will have to sell more T-shirts before it makes a profit. The margin of safety could still remain the same, but planned total sales would have to increase.

This is a good response because the student has identified that the margin of safety can remain the same, but the number of sales would have to increase.

Now try this

Explain what would happen to the break-even point in the following circumstances:

(a) The rent on Creating Together's factory premises increased.

(b) There was a fall in the cost of cloth used in the production of the T-shirts.

Remember to distinguish between a fixed cost and a variable cost.

Completing a cash flow forecast

You may be asked to complete a cash flow forecast, using simple addition and subtraction to complete each column.

Links To revise cash flow forecasts, see page 39.

Stella and Ida have started to prepare a cash flow forecast for the next three months.

Complete the cash flow forecast for Creating Together by putting figures in all the blank boxes.

£7000 is the difference between the cash coming into the enterprise in June (£15000) and the amount of cash leaving the business in June (£8000).

Sample response extract

£14750 is the total amount of cash leaving the enterprise in July.

Cash flow forecast for Creating Together for June–August 2018

2018	June (£)	July (£)	Aug (£)
Total receipts	15000	17000	12000
Total payments	8000	14750	15000
Net inflow/outflow	7000	2250	3000
Opening balance	2000	9000	11250
Closing balance	9000	11250	8250

£12000 is the total amount of cash coming into the enterprise in August.

£8250 is the closing cash balance in August, which will be the opening balance in September.

£9000 is the total amount of cash in the business at the end of June, taking into account how much cash it had at the start of the month (£2000) and the net cash inflow (£7000).

This is a good response because the student has used their knowledge of a cash flow forecast to show that:
• Net inflow/outflow = Total receipts − Total payments
• The closing balance of one month is the opening balance of the following month.

Cash flow problems

You may be asked to analyse cash flow information and suggest improvements to cash flow problems.

Links To revise analysis of cash flow information, cash flow problems and forecasting, and ways to improve cash flow, see pages 40–42.

Now try this

Prepare the next three months' cash flow figures for Creating Together using the following information:

September: Cash inflow £14000; cash outflow £12500

October: Cash inflow £15750; cash outflow £16000

November: Cash inflow £14200; cash outflow £15800

Remember that the closing balance from one month is the opening balance for the next month.

Calculating profitability

You may be asked to compare gross profit margins and net profit margins for two different years. This involves calculating the profit margins for each of the different years.

Stella and Ida have sent you some figures from their recent statement of comprehensive income.

	2017 (£)	2018 (£)
Sales	80 000	110 000
Gross profit	20 000	22 000
Net profit	12 000	12 100

They have asked you to calculate if the enterprise's profitability targets for 2017 and 2018 have been achieved. Calculate the gross profit and net profit margins for Creating Together.

Sample response extract

Remember to show your workings.

	2017		2018	
	Target	Actual	Target	Actual
Gross profit margin	22%	25% Gross profit margin $= \dfrac{20\,000}{80\,000} \times 100 = 25\%$	30%	20% Gross profit margin $= \dfrac{22\,000}{110\,000} \times 100 = 20\%$
Net profit margin	12%	15% Net profit margin $= \dfrac{12\,000}{80\,000} \times 100 = 15\%$	15%	11% Net profit margin $= \dfrac{12\,100}{110\,000} \times 100 = 11\%$

The formulas for gross profit and net profit margins will be given in the assessment.

 Links To revise profitability ratios, see pages 34 and 35, where you will find the gross profit and net profit formulas. In the assessment, you may be asked to calculate liquidity – you can revise liquidity ratios on page 36.

Comment on Creating Together's profitability by comparing 2017 to 2018.

Sample response extract

In 2017, gross and net profit margins exceeded targets but in 2018 the targets were not met. For example, in 2017 the actual gross profit margin was 25% against a target of 22% but in 2018 the actual gross profit margin was 20% against a target of 30%. This is because profit margins fell in 2018. For example, in 2017 the actual net profit margin was 15% but this fell to 11% in 2018.

 This is a good response because the student has used the data in the table to support their conclusions.

Note that the student has not used all the data from the table but has selected the data that confirms their conclusions.

Now try this

Suggest **two** reasons why Creating Together's did not meet its gross profit margin and net profit margin targets in 2018.

 Even if sales revenue increases, profit margins can still fall.

Had a look ☐   Nearly there ☐   Nailed it! ☐

Justifying a recommendation

Once you have calculated and compared an enterprise's profitability ratios, you may need to recommend whether or not you think profitability could be improved through spending more money on promotional methods. Remember to justify your recommendation.

Links Refer to the profitability ratios and comparisons you made on page 62.

Stella and Ida are concerned that their profit margins in 2018 have not met the targets. They have asked you to present your views on <u>whether or not</u> they should spend more money on promoting the new range of clothing.

Write a note to Stella and Ida justifying your recommendations

There is no one correct answer to this question. You could argue in favour of spending more money on promotional activities or against spending more money.

The skill you need to show in your response is to present a logically consistent argument to justify whichever recommendation you choose.

Sample response extract

The aim of promotions is to generate additional sales. At the same time, it needs to be remembered that promotional activities may result in additional costs and extra expenses for the enterprise. These would reduce the business's net profit margin. However, if the increase in sales revenue is greater than the cost of the promotion, then the additional cost could be justified.

This response is in favour of spending more money on promotional activities.

The response recognises that promotional activities are a cost to the enterprise, but justifies spending the additional money on promotion if it generates more revenue than the costs.

Sample response extract

Promotion is likely to result in additional costs to the enterprise which will reduce net profit margin since this is affected by the enterprise's expenses. The risk is that the additional costs of promotion will not be covered by an increase in revenue. This could be the case, for example, if the products on offer are not meeting the requirements of the consumer. Stella and Ida could consider cost-effective ways of promoting their product range.

This response is against spending more money on promotional activities.

Like the response above, it recognises that promotional activities are a cost to the enterprise, but argues that it may be too risky to spend this money on promotion and should look for more creative ways of promoting its product range which require little or no increase in costs.

Now try this

Some promotional activities can get an enterprise positive publicity without the enterprise paying for the publicity directly. Identify **two** promotional activities that would not involve additional costs for Creating Together.

Think of the role of the media in a promotional campaign.

Links To revise public relations, see page 7.

Choosing promotional methods

You may need to review the promotional mix of the enterprise. This could involve summarising an advantage and a disadvantage of different promotional methods. You may need also to identify what factors influence an enterprise's decision when choosing which methods to use.

 Links Revise choice of sales promotion methods on page 5.

Stella and Ida are reviewing Creating Together's promotional mix for its new range of clothing. They have chosen two promotional methods, and have asked you to produce a summary of the advantages and disadvantages of both:

- Send out mail order catalogues.
- Use direct mail.

Identify one advantage and one disadvantage for each of these promotional methods.

Suitability of promotional methods

You may be asked to consider the suitability of promotional methods by considering aspects such as the target audience and the product's value.

 Links Revise the factors influencing the choice of promotional methods on page 13.

Links To revise direct marketing, see page 8.

Sample response extract

Mail order catalogues

Advantage – convenient for the customer.

Disadvantage – lack of personal contact with the customer.

Direct mail

Advantage – the enterprise can target specific groups.

Disadvantage – can be annoying for the consumer to receive unwanted mail.

Direct mail is also called 'junk mail'.

The student has clearly distinguished between the advantages and disadvantage of each promotional method.

Identify two factors Stella and Ida should consider when deciding which promotional method to use.

The student has correctly identified two factors. They could also have suggested appropriateness for product or the target market. Since the question only asked for identification of two factors, identifying four factors would not receive additional marks.

Sample response extract

1 Size of promotional budget
2 Likely impact on sales

 Links Revise Choosing promotional methods on page 13.

Now try this

Why are an enterprise's brands and its public image important to its success?

Consider the long-term impact on sales revenue.

 Links To revise public relations methods and activities, see page 7.

Recommending promotional methods

You may be asked to recommend a suitable promotional method or medium to the enterprise. Think about the benefits of the method or medium, how consumers may react to it and the potential impact on the enterprise's sales.

Justifying a recommendation

When asked to recommend a particular promotional method or medium, link together a chain of related points to justify how your recommendation could improve the enterprise's performance.

Your recommendation needs to show how the money spent on a promotional activity can be justified. For example, it might improve the performance of the enterprise by increasing **sales revenue**. This could increase **profits**, which could be used to invest in new products.

| Your recommendation | → | Explain the benefits of your recommendation | → | Explain the impact that your recommendation is likely to have on the enterprise's sales, revenue or profits |

Stella and Ida have decided to advertise their new range of clothing for 16–21-year-olds. They have asked you to recommend the most effective way that they could use to reach their target market.

This extract from a response is good because it shows an understanding of the 'message' in advertising and how Creating Together could influence the purchasing habits of 16–21-year-olds (the target market).

The use of social media is one medium the enterprise could use to get its message across to consumers in its target market. Social media is widely used by 16–21-year-olds through social networking sites accessed via smartphones, tablets and laptops, which are regarded as everyday necessities by many 16–21 year olds. This may mean that the 'message' is spread via 'viral marketing'. This would increase the potential of increasing sales at a relatively low cost to the enterprise, which could have a positive impact on profi t margins.

By recommending the use of social media to communicate this message the student has recognised the lifestyle and demographics of the enterprise's target market.

The student has used specialist terms such as 'viral marketing' and 'social media'.

Notice how the final sentence in the extract is directly related to the enterprise's performance – increasing sales, low costs and increased profits.

Now try this

Explain one other promotional method that could be used to promote the new clothing range in the target market.

You need to think creatively about how promotional methods can be used in the target market.

🔗 **Links** To revise the promotional mix, see pages 1–13.

Answers

1. The promotional mix

Suggested methods of promotion may include:
- trainers: advertising, sales promotion, personal selling, direct marketing
- headphones: advertising, sales promotion, direct marketing.

2. Advertising: message and medium

The target market for the advert is primarily *young people* and those who want to listen to music 'on the go'. The 'message' is focused upon *free music* and the *convenience of access* via *mobile technology* such as smartphones.

3. Advertising: methods

Factors to take into account include:
- Local radio may be cheaper than national radio stations.
- The target market of the radio station – need to choose a radio station that is popular with 16–20-year-olds.
- The listening habits of 16–20-year-olds – they may be at school, college or at work during the day.
- The number of listeners to the radio station – if the number of listeners is low, then this will impact on the potential sales arising from the advert.

4. Sales promotion: purpose and methods

Factors could include:
- costs of the promotion and the impact on profit margins (in other words the amount of profit made by selling each greeting card)
- impact of the promotion – at this stage in the business it is important to attract customers and boost sales
- resources available to support the promotion – Lisa is unlikely to be able to use a method of promotion that requires additional resources such as a computer-based loyalty programme.

5. Sales promotion: choosing methods

Sales promotion methods could include:
(a) Discounts including buy one get one free for items with low profit margins, such as T-shirts and socks.
(b) Discounts and incentives, including money off the list price and free upgrades; a prize draw.

6. Choosing promotional methods

Ways to reduce the budget for promotional leaflets could include:
- Find an enterprise that could print the promotional flyers or leaflets more cheaply.
- Maximise the use of social media.
- Contact the local college to find out if students could design promotional leaflets as part of their course assessment.
- Print fewer leaflets, but put them in more public places such as libraries, shops, community centres, educational establishments and local takeaways and restaurants.

7. Personal selling

Qualities may include: good product knowledge, effective communicator, good listener, excellent customer service skills, persuasive, reliable.

8. Public relations

The restaurant could support the charity's fund-raising event by offering: a cash donation, a prize for the raffle such as a free meal in the restaurant, to serve food at the event at a discounted price, to put a poster advertising the event in the restaurant window.

9. Direct marketing

Direct marketing methods that Summertime Garden Centres could use include:
- Email and texts – the enterprise will have access to customer emails from the 24/7 online shopping service.
- Catalogue – this is useful for showcasing the wide range of products on offer and can also be linked to the online shopping service.
- Magazine – the 'Gardeners Enquiry Service' indicates that customers are raising queries about their gardening problems. An online magazine could cover common enquiries and problems raised by gardeners and promote products sold by the company.

10. Targeting markets

Examples may include: competitions to name a product, vote for a favourite product or win a free product.

11. Segmenting the market

Segments could include:
- Psychographic segmentation: attitudes and lifestyle – target those consumers who could be attracted to purchase an electric car because they cause less pollution.
- Demographic segmentation: consumers with high income levels who can afford expensive cars (likely to be older consumers).
- Behavioural segmentation: benefits expected from the purchase – high-income city dwellers who do not wish to use public transport but want the current convenience of electric cars for short, city centre journeys.

12. Demographic and geographic segments

Promotional methods include: leaflets advertising the restaurant distributed to households in the local area; notices and leaflets in community venues used by older citizens, parents and young people. The restaurant could use social media to target younger consumers.

13. Psychographic and behavioural segments

Psychographic characteristics may include:
- personality: willing to try new products that fit in with lifestyle
- likes and dislikes: likes healthy food
- values, attitudes and lifestyle: keen on healthy living
- interests: may take part in sporting activities.

14. Financial documents

A credit note provides details of money owed to the customer by the supplier – for example, the customer may have returned damaged goods. If the credit note is not completed accurately, then the supplier could credit the customer with either too much or too little money. If the supplier credits too much money to the customer they will lose money; if the supplier credits too little it may impact on future orders, because the customer will lose trust in the supplier and may advise others not to buy from the supplier.

15. Accuracy of financial documents

Suggested ways:
- It could manually copy all its financial documents and store them in a secure location elsewhere.
- It could regularly back-up computerised documents, and save these to a secure location.

16. Purchase order

Lemonade: 7 cases @ £4.20 per case = 7 × £4.20 = £29.40
Orange: 4 cases @ £4 per case = 4 × £4.00 = £16.00
Goods total = £29.40 + £16.00 = £45.40
Discount @ 10% = £4.54
Subtotal = £45.40 − £4.54 = £40.86
VAT @ 20% = £8.17
Total to pay = £40.86 + £8.17 = £49.03

17. Delivery note and invoice

A purchase order is a legally binding document that specifies the details of the product or services that the supplier will provide. This might include a description of the items, their quantity and when they will be delivered. A purchase order number is unique to the purchasing company, so it is important for a supplier to include it on its invoice so that the purchasing company can cross-reference it against its records and easily confirm that the supplier has delivered what has been agreed.

18. Receipt and credit note

Braddock Soft Drinks
Unit 10
Century Way Anytown AN30 1XX
RECEIPT No 23657/EP

Sent to: Eatin Pizzas   Receipt date: 17/1/18

Catalogue No	Description	Ordered	Price per case		Total cost	
			£	p	£	p
23478/LM	Lemonade	7	4	20	29	40
59352/OR	Orange	4	4	00	16	00
				Total	45	40
			Discount at 10%		4	54
			Total excluding VAT		40	86
			VAT @ 20%		8	17
			Total paid in full		49	03

19. Payment methods

Suggested differences between a credit card and a debit card:
- Debit card: money is taken directly out of a person's bank account. Credit card: a form of instant loan.
- Debit card: the amount owing is taken from the cardholder's current account immediately. Credit card: the amount borrowed attracts interest after a certain period of time.

20. Choice of payment methods

(a) cash or contactless debit card (low-cost purchase; café may not accept card payments)
(b) direct debit (mobile phone bills may differ in amounts each month)
(c) credit card (person may have insufficient funds or might want an interest-free period)

21. Income

It could raise income through:
- renting out part of its premises to another enterprise, such as a car hire company or a garage repair business
- leasing or hiring vehicles to customers
- using some of its surplus cash from its profits to invest in another car enterprise.

22. Costs

Fixed costs: (d)
Variable costs: (a), (b), (c)

23. Financial terminology

Examples include:
(a) leather, shoe dye, laces
(b) heating and lighting
(c) factory; machinery; company vehicles; cash in the bank
(d) suppliers of leather
(e) shoe shops.

24. Turnover, cost of sales and gross profit

1 Cost of sales per pair of jeans = £8
   Cost of sales per month = £8 × 175 = £1400
2 Turnover:
   January: 175 × £20 = £3500
   February:
   1st sale: 100 × £20 = £2000
   £2000 × 5% = £100 (discount to be applied)
   So
   £2000 − £100 = £1900
   2nd sale: 75 × £20 = £1500
   Total sales = £1900 + £1500 = £3400
3 Gross profit:
   January: £3500 − £1400 = £2100
   February: £3400 − £1400 = £2000

25. Profit and expenses

(a) Gross profit could be increased by increasing revenue or reducing the cost of sales.
(b) Net profit could be increased by reducing business expenses.

26. Fixed and current assets

Current assets: inventory £2000, cash in bank £4000, money owed by customers £3250.
Total value of current assets = £9250
Fixed assets: van £4000, computers £2500, other office equipment £2000.
Total value of fixed assets = £8500

27. Liabilities, debtors and creditors

Short-term liabilities (overdraft, short-term loan, trade credit) = £2000 + £1500 + £2500 = £6000
Long-term liabilities (bank loan, mortgage) = £6000 + £40000 + £46000

28. Capital and net current assets

Net current assets = Current assets − Current liabilities
= £7500 − £4500 = £3000
The value of net current assets is positive which means that the business has sufficient current assets to meet its current liabilities.

29. Statement of comprehensive income

	£	£
Sales		30 000
Cost of sales		6 000
Gross profit		**24 000**
Less expenses		
Wages	10 000	
Rent	5 000	
Transport	1 600	
Marketing	1 500	
Insurance	750	
	18 850	
Net profit		5 150

30. Profit or loss

Net profit = Gross profit − Expenses
Gross profit = £35 450 − £12 250 = £23 200
Net profit = £23 200 − £8 400 = £14 800

31. Statement of financial position (1)

1 current liability: either the overdraft of £200 or the £800 owed to suppliers
2 Net current assets = Current assets − Current liabilities
   = £5300 − £1000 = £4300

32. Statement of financial position (2)

Statement of financial position as of 31 December 2018		
	£	£
Fixed assets		
Computer	1 000	
Vehicles	3 000	
		4 000
Current assets		
Inventory (stock)	45 000	
Debtors (trade receivables)	30 000	
Cash in bank	3 000	
		78 000
Current liabilities		
Creditors (trade payables)	34 000	
Overdraft	15 000	
		49 000
Net current assets		
Total assets *less* current liabilities		33 000
Financed by		
Owners capital	20 000	
Retained profit	13 000	
		33 000

- The enterprise has made a profit of £13 000 (positive – however, we don't know if this is an increase or decrease on the previous year).
- Net current assets total is £33 000 (positive – however, the enterprise only has £3000 in cash and this could be a problem given that it has £34 000 of outstanding bills (creditors). The situation could be made worse if some of the money owed by the enterprise's debtors (£30 000) is not paid on time – or not paid at all).
- The enterprise needs to increase the amount of cash it has by:
- ensuring its debtors pay their bills on time
- selling some of its inventory (stock) for cash.

33. Cash, profit, liquidity and profitability

Profit considers total revenue and total costs. This is important because the enterprise must always ensure that it generates more revenue than it spends. Profitability is important because it considers how much profit is being made on each sale (or each £ of sales revenue). The enterprise needs to ensure that it generates as much profit as possible from each sale because if it does, its total profit will increase.

34. Profitability ratios (1)

Gross profit margin $= \dfrac{16\,640}{20\,800} \times 100 = 80\%$

35. Profitability ratios (2)

Net profit margin $= \dfrac{5200}{20\,800} \times 100 = 25\%$

36. Liquidity ratios

(a) Current ratio $= \dfrac{£77\,000}{£56\,000} = 1.37{:}1$
The enterprise should be able to pay its short-term debts.

(b) Liquid capital ratio $= \dfrac{£77\,000 - £22\,000}{£56\,000} = 0.98{:}1$

This shows the enterprise has insufficient assets to cover its short-term debt. It needs to be able to sell some of its inventory (stock). This shows the enterprise may struggle to pay its short-term debts because it does not have enough cash. It would be advised to reduce the quantity of inventory (stock) and increase its cash levels.

37. Cash, sales and purchases

Money held in a bank account is cash which is the most liquid of all assets. The risk to the enterprise with invoices owed by customers is that they may take a long time to pay or may not pay at all.

38. Cash flow

Cash inflows: cash sales of £25 000.

39. Cash flow forecasts

Closing balance for March = £7555
So opening balance for April = £7555
Total receipts = £3200
Total payments = £2350
Closing balance = £7555 + £3200 − £2350 = £8405

40. Analysis of cash flow information

Closing balance = Opening balance + Cash inflows − Cash outflows
= £230 + £6000 − £6400 = (£170)

41. Cash flow problems and forecasting

If sales targets are over-ambitious, it is likely that they will not be met. As a result, the enterprise's cash flow statement at the end of the period would show that the business had experienced a cash flow problem. It is likely that the business would then have to take action during this period to address the cash flow problem, either by reducing cash outflows or finding ways in which to increase cash inflows.

42. Improving cash flow

If an enterprise has to wait a long time to be paid, it may mean that it does not have sufficient reserves of cash to pay its monthly bills, such as labour costs, rent and any interest payments on business loans. It will therefor experience cash flow difficulties.

43. Break-even

(a) Break-even point $= \dfrac{£5400}{£80 - £20} = 90$ units

(b) Break-even point $= \dfrac{£5400}{£110 - £20} = 60$ units

44. Break-even charts

Any two from: fixed costs, variable costs, total costs, total revenue (sales), selling price of product.

45. Interpreting a break-even chart

The difference between the planned sales/output and the break-even point is known as the margin of safety. This shows how far sales could fall before they would affect the enterprise's ability to cover its costs. A small margin of safety could be risky as it would leave the enterprise open to financial difficulties – if sales fell, its total revenue would fall. If sales continued to fall, total revenue could fall to a level below the break-even point, at which stage the enterprise would be making a loss.

46. Using break-even analysis in planning

1 Increasing the selling price will lower the break-even point. This could offset the rise in costs.
2 The risk is that fewer customers will visit the restaurant if prices increase.

47. Limitations of break-even analysis

Suggested impacts may include:
- Import prices could increase, resulting in an increase in variable costs, which would increase the break-even point.
- The government could increase the hourly rate of the living wage, resulting in an increase in variable costs, which would increase the break-even point.
- The enterprise may be able to negotiate a discount for buying components in bulk, which would result in a decrease in variable costs and a fall in the break-even point.

48. The need for business finance

Suggested reasons include:
- The person may lack business experience.
- The market may contain a lot of enterprises producing similar products.
- The person may not have produced a detailed business plan covering such features as breakdown of costs and revenue and a break-even analysis.

49. Internal sources of finance

The enterprise may intend to reinvest the retained profit in the business rather than to rely on a loan which would require it to pay interest charges.

50. External sources of finance – short term

Trade credit is offered by suppliers in order to generate additional sales from business customers. The risk to the supplier is that the customer may not pay for the supplies they have received or they may take longer than the credit terms agreed, resulting in cash flow problems for the supplier.

51. External sources of finance – long term

(a) trade credit
(b) leasing
(c) venture capital; peer-to-peer lending; bank loan
(d) government grant; venture capital; peer-to-peer lending; bank loan

52. Your Component 3 set task

Student's own response.

53. Understanding a scenario

The target market will influence the types of promotional activities that will make up the promotional mix. In the case of Creating Together, the target market for its new range of clothing is 16–21-year-olds. Knowing the demographics of this age group (including their spending habits and their income levels) will determine the types of promotional activities that will entice consumers to buy. Promotional methods include coupons, competitions and loyalty incentives which can influence brand recognition, loyalty and sales.
Promotion must provide the enterprise with value for money by leading to increased sales. Identifying the target market ensures that money spent on promotions is targeted towards the group and not wasted on promotional activities that do not reach the target group.

54. Understanding financial information

An invoice would be needed.

55. Identifying financial information

A catalogue number or stock number helps to identify a specific product so it can be distinguished from other products. These features could include colour, size and price. A catalogue or stock number is a useful reference point when a customer checks their invoice for accuracy. An incorrect catalogue number or stock number could result in the wrong amount being calculated on the invoice.

56. Completing a financial document

To complete the invoice you need to calculate 20 per cent of £921.50.

$$\text{VAT} = \frac{20}{100} \times £921.50 = \frac{1}{5} \times £921.50 = \frac{£921.50}{5} = £184.30$$

Total to pay = £921.50 + £184.30 = £1105.80

57. Completing a statement of financial position

Assets = Current liabilities + Long-term liabilities + Owner's capital
£15 500 = £1500 + Long-term liabilities + £8000
Therefore, long-term liabilities = £15 500 − (£1500 + £8000) = £15 500 − £9500 = £6000

58. Suggesting appropriate actions

Suggested advantages include:
- attract more customers
- increase market share
- free up warehouse space (reduce inventory)
- meet business targets
- build a reputation and brand.

59. Drawing a break-even chart

At 700 unit sales:
Variable costs = 700 × £5 = £3500
Total revenue = 700 × £10 = £7000
Total costs = £2000 + (700 × £5) = £2000 + £3500 = £5500
Profit = Total revenue − Total costs = £7000 − £5500 = £1500

60. Interpreting break-even charts

(a) Rent is a fixed cost, so the fixed cost line would move upwards, resulting in an *increase* in the break-even point.
(b) Cloth is a variable cost and a reduction in variable costs would result in a *fall* in the break-even point (the variable cost line would become less steep).

61. Completing a cash flow forecast

Cash flow forecast for Creating Together for September–November 2018			
2018	Sept (£)	Oct (£)	Nov (£)
Total receipts	14 000	15 750	14 200
Total payments	12 500	16 000	15 800
Net inflow/ outflow	1 500	(250)	(1,600)
Opening balance	8 250	9 750	9 500
Closing balance	9 750	9 500	7 900

62. Calculating profitability

Suggested reasons for the missed targets in 2018 include the following:
- Cost of sales could have increased.
- Business expenses could have increased.
- Changes in price or the inventory level.
- The targets may have been over-ambitious.

63. Justifying a recommendation

Suggested promotional activities without direct cost to Creating Together:
- use of social media
- press releases
- sponsorship.

64. Choosing promotional methods

An enterprise's brands and public image can persuade customers and potential customers to buy its products and services. This may result in an increase in sales and sales revenue. Brands and corporate image can also have a positive impact upon customer loyalty, encouraging customers to keep buying its products.

65. Recommending promotional methods

Attendance at music festivals and other music venues attended by 16–21 year olds – this could include 'pop-up' stores selling discounted T-shirts and clothing, which would allow face-to-face contact with people in the target market. If the T-shirts were promoted by celebrity musicians, it could influence the brand image and, with it, future sales.

Notes

Notes

Notes

Notes

Notes

Notes